250 ESSENTIAL KANJI
FOR EVERYDAY USE

VOLUME ONE

250
ESSENTIAL KANJI FOR EVERYDAY USE

生活の中の漢字

VOLUME ONE

KANJI TEXT RESEARCH GROUP
UNIVERSITY OF TOKYO

TUTTLE PUBLISHING
Boston • Rutland, Vermont • Tokyo

Publication of this book was assisted by a grant from the Japan Foundation.

Published by Tuttle Publishing,
an imprint of Periplus Editions (HK) Ltd.,
with editorial offices at 153 Milk Street, Boston, Massachusetts 02109.

LCC Card No. 93-60664
ISBN 0-8048-3558-6

First edition, 1993

Printed in Singapore

Distributed by:

Japan
Tuttle Publishing
Yaekari Building, 3rd Floor
5-4-12 Osaki, Shinagawa-ku
Tokyo 141-0032
Tel: (03) 5437 0171; Fax: (03) 5437 0755
Email: tuttle-sales@gol.com

North America, Latin America & Europe
Tuttle Publishing
364 Innovation Drive
North Clarendon, VT 05759-9436
Tel: (802) 773 8930; Fax: (802) 773 6993
Email: info@tuttlepublishing.com
www.tuttlepublishing.com

Asia Pacific
Berkeley Books Pte. Ltd.
130 Joo Seng Road, #06-01/03
Singapore 368357
Tel: (65) 6280 1330; Fax: (65) 6280 6290
Email: inquiries@periplus.com.sg

08 07 06 05 04
14 13 12 11 10 9

To the Learners

Welcome to ESSENTIAL KANJI FOR EVERYDAY USE. How do you feel about studying kanji? These exotic and alien characters are all around you as you go about your daily life in Japan, and at first they may seem impossible to learn. Well, they're not. If you start by becoming familiar with kanji encountered on a daily basis, you'll feel much more comfortable in Japan. You'll no longer have to walk down the street oblivious to written warnings, no longer miss out on sales because you couldn't read the advertisements, and no longer be in social and cultural limbo because of an inability to read entertainment listings.

ESSENTIAL KANJI FOR EVERYDAY USE will teach you the 250 kanji that most frequently appear in daily life. Each of the following 21 lessons illustrates situations in places you are likely to find yourself in Japan: train stations, banks, post offices, restaurants, hospitals, and university campuses. All the tools you need to feel comfortable and accomplish your goals in these environments are right here in this book.

Each lesson is divided into an exercise section and a kanji section. The quizzes found in the exercise section will help you learn the kanji and kanji compounds that relate to the situations presented in the text. The kanji charts introduce new characters and information about them. To help you understand and remember the kanji, etymologies or memory-aids have been included.

There you have it—250 of the most important kanji for starting your reading life in Japan. After completing your study of the kanji in this textbook, you should feel quite at home in various everyday situations. We sincerely hope that this guide will make your life in Japan both easier and more enjoyable.

July, 1993

Kanji Text Research Group
Japanese Language Class
Department of Civil Engineering
University of Tokyo

Akiyo Nishino
Junko Ishida
Kazuko Nagatomi
Junko Sagara
Masako Watanabe
Yoshiko Yamazaki

はじめに

本書の目的と特徴

本書は、日本語学習者（特に非漢字圏）が日常生活に役立つ250の漢字を、生活の場所や場面を通して学ぶための初歩の漢字の学習書である。またさらには、将来、より進んだ漢字学習へつなげることも目指している。そして、何よりも、興味を持って楽しく学ばせることが本書のねらいである。

来日当初より、駅での表示や交通標識、銀行や郵便局等の窓口、あるいは店や食堂、その他の場所で使われている漢字を目にして、意味が理解できずに困ることが多い。生活空間で目にする漢字の意味が分かれば、日本での生活が容易になる。また、生活に役立つ漢字を覚えれば、繰り返しその漢字に接することになるので、学習した漢字が無理なく定着する。そして、その後の漢字学習に対して意欲を増すようになるだろう。このように考えて、本書では課ごとに上記のような場面を設定し、そこに現れる漢字を課題を通して学習できるように工夫した。

本書で取り上げた漢字には、一つ一つに対して、成立ちあるいは覚え方のヒントを示した。これは漢字の形と意味の関連を具体的に知ることによって、記憶がより容易になり、漢字学習が楽しくなるようにと考えたためである。原則として成立ちの説明は従来の説に従ったが、初心者にとって難しいものには代わりに覚え方のヒントを新たに考えた。また、個々の漢字の持つ意味だけではなく、その漢字を使った熟語も紹介した。熟語を学習することによって、一つの漢字がほかの漢字と結びついて新しい熟語を構成するという漢字の造語力に気づかせ、応用力を身につけることを期待している。

本書は、教室で教材として用いることも、独習用のテキストとしても使用することもできる。

本書作成の背景

本書は、もともと東京大学大学院工学系研究科土木工学専攻の留学生のための初級漢字教育の教科書として作成されたものである。土木工学専攻では、1982年10月から留学生に対して日英二か国語を使用言語とし、日英どちらでも学位が取れる態勢を整えた。学生は英語で専門教育が受けられるようになり、学業のための日本語は必要としなくなった。しかし、学生が大学内外で円滑に生活できるようにするために、土木工学専攻では独自に日本語教育を始めた。

漢字教育もその一部である。はじめは日本語の教科書に沿って漢字を教えていたが、上記の日本語教育の目的に添うように、新たに、学生の身のまわりの言葉を場面ごとに分類した "KANJI AND KATAKANA AROUND YOU" を作った。その中から必要度が高いと思われる500の漢字を選んで、"EASY WAY TO KANJI" を1988年5月に作成し、漢字教科書として使い始めた。1989年度には文部省から教育方法等改善費が与えられ、それを機会に改めて250の漢字を選択し、生活の場面に応じて分類した上、クイズも加えて「生活の中の漢字」を作成した。本書は、この「生活の中の漢字」をもとに、当教室の学生だけではなく、生活のために漢字の学習を必要としている一般の学習者にも役立つようにさらに改訂したものである。

作成過程

東京大学土木工学専攻の日本語教室の学生（留学生、研究員、教官とかれらの配偶者）を対象に、漢字を必要とする場面についてインタビューやアンケート調査を行った。その結果に基づいて、いろいろな場所へ学生と一緒に出かけて行き、生活に必要な漢字の写真を撮った。

さらにそれらの写真に加えて、銀行での手続きや定期券の購入などに必要な用紙、食堂のメニュー、大学の諸手続きの用紙類を集めた。学生の意見や彼らが生活の中でメモをした漢字のリスト、留学生の世話をする日本人学生に対するアンケート調査なども資料として、場面別の漢字熟語リストを作った。それらを参考に、学生が日本で生活する上で必要と思われる21の場面と250の漢字

を選び出した。漢字の選定に当たっては、必要度、資料の中での使用頻度、そして、個々の漢字の造語力を考慮した。各場面は、イラストや実物のサンプル、写真などで構成し、その場面で遭遇するであろう問題に対して適切な行動がとれるような課題をつけた。

本書の構成と使い方

　本書は、各場面を一課として21課から成り立っている。各課は、タイトルページ、1. Introductory Quiz（場面と質問）、2. Vocabulary（語彙表）、3. New Characters（新出漢字）、4. Practice（練習問題）、5. Supplement（補足）から構成されている。そしていくつかの課ごとにReview Exercise（復習問題）のページを設けた。巻末には、付録、解答、音訓索引と熟語索引をつけた。タイトルページにはその課で扱われている場面の写真や実物のサンプルおよび簡単な文化的背景をつけた。21課のうち第10課までは、全ての文を分ち書きにした。1. から 5. を通して、原則として未習の漢字と、本書で学ぶ250字以外の漢字にはふりがなを載せた。2. と 3. では、250字以外の漢字の上には ✕ 印をつけた。なお、ローマ字の表記は原則としてヘボン式を使用した。

各課の構成と使い方は以下の通りである。

1. INTRODUCTORY QUIZ（場面と質問）

　日常生活で出会う場面のイラストと質問 (quiz)からなる。まず、2. の語彙表を参照しながら、イラストの中のことばの読み方と意味を知る。次に質問に答えることにより、提示された場面の内容を理解する。ここでは、学習者が実生活で遭遇するであろう場面を目にすることによって学習意欲が湧き、場面に結びつけて漢字やことばの意味を理解することを目的としている。漢字を学習した後にもう一度語彙表を見ずにやってみることをすすめる。教室では実生活での経験をまじえて日頃の疑問点などを話し合うのも効果的であろう。

2. VOCABULARY（語彙表）

　場面と質問で使われていることばの読み方と意味が載せてある。イラストの理解や、質問に答えるときに参照してほしい。漢字の上の数字はその漢字を学習する課を示す。 ✕ 印の漢字は250字に含まれていない。

3. NEW CHARACTERS（新出漢字）

　新出漢字のリストと漢字チャートからなる。チャートには新出漢字一つ一つについて、漢字の意味、基本的な音訓読み、書き順、成立ちや覚え方のヒント、熟語とその英訳が載せてある。熟語欄には、原則として新出漢字と既習漢字との組合せによってできたことばを上段に載せた。下段には、そのほか日常生活でよく使用されることばを載せた。教室では上段のみを扱い、余裕のある学習者には下段も勉強することをすすめる。送りがなは慣用的なものを重視し、本来のものは （ ） の中に入れて示した。この 3. では、新出漢字の記憶を確かなものにするとともに、応用範囲を広げることを目的としている。

4. PRACTICE（練習問題）

　まとめとして、漢字の読み書きを練習する。出題の対象となっていることばは、3. の熟語欄の上段のもので、下段のものは扱っていない。解答はついていないので、その課のチャートで確認してほしい。

5. SUPPLEMENT（補足）

　課によって、その課の場面に関連のある用紙類のサンプルや写真などを補足としてつけ加えた。

　本書の出版に当たって、多くの方々にお世話になった。細部にわたってご教示をくださった杏林大学教授伊藤芳照先生をはじめ、日本語教育関係の方々から貴重なコメントやご支援をいただいた。

　また、各方面の方々に、資料の提供など様々なご協力をいただいた。イラストは東京大学の卒業生で、現在宇都宮大学工学部建設学科池田裕一氏が引き受けてくださった。土木工学専攻の教職員や日本人学生諸氏には、特に、DTPによる版下作成など協力をしてもらった。本書の出版を期待し、本書の作成過程においていろいろな面で協力してくれた留学生諸氏を含め、心からお礼申し上げたい。

　個々の漢字の成立ちに関しては、藤堂明保編の小学館刊「例解学習漢字辞典」と学習研究社刊「漢字源」を主に参考にさせていただいた。

　最後になったが、この本を世に出してくださったチャールズ・イー・タトル出版社、特に編集担当ケン・モリ・ウォン氏、英語の訂正をしてくださったサリー・シュワガー氏に深く感謝申し上げる。お二人には、本を作成する上で、いろいろな貴重なコメントをいただいた。

　この本を教科書や自習用テキストとして使っていただき、率直なご批評やご感想をいただければ幸いである。

　また、チャールズ・イー・タトル出版社は、本書の出版にあたり、国際交流基金日本語センターの日本語教材作成助成を受けることができた。著者としても、ここで感謝の意を表したい。

1993年7月

東京大学大学院工学系研究科
土木工学専攻日本語教室
漢字教材研究グループ

西　野　章　代
石　田　順　子
長　富　和　子
相　良　淳　子
渡　辺　雅　子
山　崎　佳　子

Contents

THE LESSONS

Lesson	Subjects Covered	Kanji Introduced	Page
1 なにか たべましょう Let's Eat	Numerals, prices	一 二 三 四 五 六 七 八 九 十 百 円	21
2 スキーに いきます Going Skiing	Time, dates	休 月 日 週 間 千 万 午 前 後 時 半 分	29
3 きょうは なん曜日ですか What Day Is Today?	Days of the week	曜 火 水 木 金 土 平 成 年 祝 祭	39
4 はじめまして、どうぞよろしく How Do You Do?	University majors, street addresses	大 学 東 京 留 生 工 部 科 専 攻 先 本 語 都 市 入 式 文 区 丁 目	47
5 定期券を かいます Buying a Commuter's Pass	Application forms	定 期 券 申 込 書 氏 名 男 女 才 駅 使 用 開 始 住 所 電 話 通	59
REVIEW EXERCISE	Lessons 1-5		72
6 なに線に のりますか Which Line Do You Take?	Subways in Tokyo	地 下 鉄 丸 内 線 代 田 手 西 営 団 新 上	73
7 きっぷを かいましょう Buying Tickets	JR tickets	山 中 央 連 絡 自 動 小 人 全 行 回	82
8 電車に のりましょう Taking the Train	Train stations	車 口 出 方 面 番	91
9 駅の 中 Inside the Station	Station facilities	北 南 案 便 洗 子 事 故 不	97
10 駅の ホーム Station Platforms	Types of trains, timetables	各 停 普 準 急 速 快 特 表 終 着 発	105
REVIEW EXERCISE	Lessons 6-10		114
11 銀行 At the Bank	ATMs	銀 引 預 押 号 暗 証 確 認 訂 正 残 高 記 帳 取 扱 止	115
12 郵便局 At the Post Office	Mailing letters and packages	郵 局 切 外 国 際 航 空 常 料 他 様	127

Lesson	Subjects Covered	Kanji Introduced	Page
13どの道を通ったらいいでしょうか Which Way Should I Go?	Road signs	道 歩 者 禁 立 注 意	137
14たばこは、どこですったらいいですか Where Can I Smoke?	Signs in public places	気 危 険 非 消 煙 左 右	145
REVIEW EXERCISE	Lessons 11-14		152
15キャンパス・マップ Campus Map	Campus facilities	講 堂 食 門 館 会 協 図 閉	153
16大学のたてものの中 In the University	University rooms	階 義 議 室 研 究 務 実 験	161
17なんのお知らせですか Announcements	Campus notices	知 場 教 見 費 院 修 士 博 明 届	169
18病院へ行きます Going to the Hospital	Medical terms, hospital units	病 医 歯 児 産 保 受 付 来 薬 診 察 計 支 払 法 毎	179
REVIEW EXERCISE	Lessons 15-18		190
19スーパーでセールがあります Shopping at the Supermarket	Shopping	店 売 肉 牛 豚 鳥 魚 割 品 安 買 物 業	191
20食堂に入りましょう Eating Out	Restaurant menus and signs	和 洋 汁 飲 茶 湯 予 約 席 備	201
21不動産屋で At the Real Estate Agency	Realtor information	屋 貸 有 無	211
REVIEW EXERCISE	Lessons 19-21		217

Introduction

This book contains 21 lessons introducing 250 kanji. Each lesson focuses on an everyday situation that you may encounter in Japan. Before Lesson 1, there is a brief introduction of kanji and kana, and after every several lessons there are review exercises. The *on-kun* index and vocabulary index are found at the end. This book is designed as a textbook for you to use both in the classroom and while studying on your own.

Organization of the Lessons

Each lesson is divided into the following sections.

The chapter title pages present pictures and cultural notes that give you a brief introduction to each lesson. From Lesson 1 through Lesson 10, the Japanese is written with a space between words. Hiragana is given alongside kanji that you have not yet learned or are not included in the basic 250 kanji. A modified Hepburn system of romanization has been used.

1 INTRODUCTORY QUIZ

This section illustrates situations that you may encounter in daily life, and is followed by a quiz. By referring first to the words in VOCABULARY, you will learn the readings and meanings of the words introduced in the lesson. Taking the quiz will lead you to an understanding of the situation presented in the illustration, and trying the quiz again after studying each kanji is a good review technique.

2 VOCABULARY

This section contains the readings and meanings of the words used in the INTRODUCTORY QUIZ, and you should refer to it when studying the illustrations or taking the quiz. The numeral above each kanji indicates the lesson where the kanji is introduced.

3 NEW CHARACTERS

This section introduces new kanji and their meanings, along with basic *on-kun* readings, stroke orders, etymologies or hints for memory-aid, and compounds with English translations. The compounds essentially consist of newly or previously introduced kanji. Kanji that are not included in the 250 taught in this book are marked with ×. More important compounds are shown in the upper part of the list; these should be taught in the classroom. However, you are encouraged to study those in the lower part of the list as well. When kana is optionally added to kanji *(okurigana)*, the most common usage is adopted and formal usages are shown in parentheses.

4 PRACTICE

This section provides practice for reading and writing the kanji in the upper part of the kanji charts. You should use the practice as a final check for the kanji learned in each lesson. Answers to the practice problems are not provided in this textbook.

5 SUPPLEMENT

Some lessons contain related supplemental information, forms and / or photographs.

Kanji

The oldest Chinese characters, the precursors of kanji, originated more than 3,000 years ago. Originally they were simple illustrations of objects and phenomena in daily life, and developed as a writing tool mainly characterized by pictography and ideography. Thus each of the Chinese characters carries its own meaning within itself.

Chinese characters, or kanji, can be classified according to origin and structure, into four categories:

1. Pictographic characters derive from the shapes of concrete objects.

    🌳 → 木 → 木 = tree

    ☀ → ⊖ → 日 = sun

2. Sign characters are composed of points and lines to express abstract ideas.

    • / — → 丄 → 上 = above, on, up

    — / • → 下 → 下 = below, under, down

3. Ideographic characters are composed of combinations of other characters.

    木 (tree) ＋ 木 (tree) → 林 = wood

    日 (sun) ＋ 月 (moon) → 明 = bright

4. Phonetic-ideographic characters are composed of combinations of ideographic and phonetic elements. Upper parts or right-hand parts often indicate the reading of the kanji. About 90% of all kanji fall into this category.

    先 (セン previous) → 洗 (セン wash)

    安 (アン peaceful) → 案 (アン proposal)

The Japanese had no writing symbols until kanji were introduced from China in the 5th century. Soon after this, kanji were simplified into phonetic symbols known as hiragana and katakana. Thus the Japanese language came to be written in combinations of kanji and kana. (See page 15)

This kanji-kana writing system is more effective than writing with kana only. As the written Japanese language doesn't leave spaces between words, kanji among kana make it easier for readers to distinguish units of meaning and to understand the context. Readers can easily grasp the rough meaning of written text by following kanji only.

Kanji can usually be read two ways. These readings are referred to as *on-yomi* and *kun-yomi*. *On-yomi* is the Japanese reading taken from the original Chinese pronunciation. *Kun-yomi* is the pronunciation of an original Japanese word applied to a kanji according to its meaning. Hiragana added after *kun-yomi* readings are called *okurigana*. *Okurigana* primarily indicate the inflectional ending of a kanji, though the last part of the stem is occasionally included in the *okurigana*.

Most kanji are composed of two or more elements, and parts of one kanji are often found in different combinations in other kanji. Certain commonly shared parts are called radicals, or *bushu* in Japanese. Radicals are used to classify kanji in dictionaries; thus each kanji is allocated only one radical. Each radical also carries a core meaning. For example, the radical 言 means "word" or "speak." Therefore the kanji 語 (language), 話 (speak, story), 読 (read), 記 (note down), and 論 (discuss), all have something to do with the meaning of 言. There are 214 radicals altogether. Some frequently seen radicals are listed below.

1. 扌 hand   2. 土 earth   3. 氵 water   4. 亻 man, people 5. 言 word, speak

6. 木 tree   7. 艹 plant   8. 糸 thread   9. 金 metal, gold 10. 辶 road, proceed

11. 儿 legs   12. 口 mouth   13. 阝 village   14. 阝 wall, hill   15. 日 sun, day

16. 門 gate   17. 尸 courpse   18. 疒 sickness   19. 宀 roof, house   20. 十 add, many

Kanji strokes are written in a fixed direction and order. There are several fundamental rules for writing the strokes.

1. horizontal strokes: from left to right

三 (three)   土 (soil)   工 (engineering)

2. vertical or slanting strokes: from top to bottom

十 (ten)   木 (tree)   人 (man)   八 (eight)

3. hook strokes: from top left to right or left bottom

日 (day)   手 (hand)   分 (minute)   氏 (surname)

4. the center stroke first, followed by the left and right strokes

小 (small)   山 (mountain)

5. the outside strokes first, followed by the middle strokes

月 (moon)   中 (inside)

6. the horizontal stroke first, followed by the vertical stroke (usually followed by another horizontal stroke)

十 (ten)   土 (soil)

7. the left-hand slanting stroke first, followed by the right-hand side

八 (eight)   六 (six)

As knowledge of kanji increases, kanji dictionaries become more helpful. In order to refer to a kanji dictionary, one of three things needs to be known about the kanji: the radical, the number of strokes, or the reading.

1. By the radical *(bushu)*:
   Look for the kanji by radical in the *bushu* index.
2. By the number of strokes *(kakusū)*:
   Look for the kanji by stroke number in the *kakusū* index.
3. By the reading:
   Look for the kanji by pronunciation in the *on-kun* reading index.

Kana

Japanese Writing Systems

There are four different kinds of characters used for writing Japanese: kanji, hiragana, katakana, and romaji (Roman alphabet). Kanji incorporate meaning as well as sounds. Hiragana, katakana, and romaji are phonetic characters that express only sounds. However, unlike English, one kana character can only be pronounced one way: 「あ」 or 「ア」 is only pronounced [a].

Japanese sentences are usually written with a combination of kanji, hiragana, and katakana. Katakana is mainly used for foreign words that are adapted to fit Japanese pronunciation. Kanji appears in nouns, verbs, adjectives, and adverbs. Hiragana is primarily used to show the inflectional endings of kanji *(okurigana)*. Particles, conjunctions, and interjections are mostly written in hiragana. Although hiragana can substitute for kanji, a combination of kanji and hiragana is much faster to read. For example:

私は毎朝早く起きます。出かける前にテレビを見ます。
わたしはまいあさはやくおきます。でかけるまえにテレビをみます。
Watashi-wa maiasa hayaku okimasu. Dekakeru mae-ni terebi-o mimasu.
I get up early every morning. I watch TV before I leave home.

Japanese Syllabary Chart

Each square □ represents one pronounced syllable.

hiragana ─┐ あ a
romaji ───┤ ア
katakana ─┘

	a	i	u	e	o
	あ a / ア	い i / イ	う u / ウ	え e / エ	お o / オ
k	か ka / カ	き ki / キ	く ku / ク	け ke / ケ	こ ko / コ
s	さ sa / サ	し shi / シ	す su / ス	せ se / セ	そ so / ソ
t	た ta / タ	ち chi / チ	つ tsu / ツ	て te / テ	と to / ト
n	な na / ナ	に ni / ニ	ぬ nu / ヌ	ね ne / ネ	の no / ノ
h	は ha / ハ	ひ hi / ヒ	ふ fu / フ	へ he / ヘ	ほ ho / ホ
m	ま ma / マ	み mi / ミ	む mu / ム	め me / メ	も mo / モ
y	や ya / ヤ		ゆ yu / ユ		よ yo / ヨ
r	ら ra / ラ	り ri / リ	る ru / ル	れ re / レ	ろ ro / ロ
w	わ wa / ワ				を o / ヲ

ya		yu		yo	
きゃ / キャ	kya	きゅ / キュ	kyu	きょ / キョ	kyo
しゃ / シャ	sha	しゅ / シュ	shu	しょ / ショ	sho
ちゃ / チャ	cha	ちゅ / チュ	chu	ちょ / チョ	cho
にゃ / ニャ	nya	にゅ / ニュ	nyu	にょ / ニョ	nyo
ひゃ / ヒャ	hya	ひゅ / ヒュ	hyu	ひょ / ヒョ	hyo
みゃ / ミャ	mya	みゅ / ミュ	myu	みょ / ミョ	myo

りゃ / リャ	rya	りゅ / リュ	ryu	りょ / リョ	ryo

ん n / ン

g	が ga ガ	ぎ gi ギ	ぐ gu グ	げ ge ゲ	ご go ゴ
z	ざ za ザ	じ ji ジ	ず zu ズ	ぜ ze ゼ	ぞ zo ゾ
d	だ da ダ	ぢ ji ヂ	づ zu ヅ	で de デ	ど do ド
b	ば ba バ	び bi ビ	ぶ bu ブ	べ be ベ	ぼ bo ボ
p	ぱ pa パ	ぴ pi ピ	ぷ pu プ	ぺ pe ペ	ぽ po ポ

ぎゃ gya ギャ	ぎゅ gyu ギュ	ぎょ gyo ギョ
じゃ ja ジャ	じゅ ju ジュ	じょ jo ジョ

びゃ bya ビャ	びゅ byu ビュ	びょ byo ビョ
ぴゃ pya ピャ	ぴゅ pyu ピュ	ぴょ pyo ピョ

Additional Katakana

Created with small ア イ ウ エ オ ュ

	a	i	u	e	o	yu
y				イェ ye		
w		ウィ wi		ウェ we	ウォ wo	
kw	クァ kwa	クィ kwi		クェ kwe	クォ kwo	
gw	グァ gwa	グィ gwi		グェ gwe	グォ gwo	
sh				シェ she		
j				ジェ je		
t		ティ ti	トゥ tu			テュ tyu
d		ディ di	ドゥ du			デュ dyu
ts	ツァ tsa	ツィ tsi		ツェ tse	ツォ tso	
f	ファ fa	フィ fi		フェ fe	フォ fo	フュ fyu
v	ヴァ va	ヴィ vi	ヴ vu	ヴェ ve	ヴォ vo	ヴュ vyu

Derivation of Kana

Hiragana and katakana are Japanese phonetic syllabary developed from kanji in the 8th century. Hiragana, which are cursive letters, derive from the shapes of entire kanji characters. Katakana, which are combinations of straight lines, derive from various parts of kanji characters. In some cases both hiragana and katakana are derived from the same kanji, such as *to*, *fu*, and *me* in the following examples. Kana derived from some of the kanji introduced in this textbook are shown on the next page.

a	安 あ あ	ha	八 八 ハ
ke	計 计 け	he	部 ゐ へ
		he	部 ゐ へ
sa	左 さ さ	ho	保 保 ほ
		ho	保 保 ホ
chi	知 ち ち	mi	三 三 ミ
chi	千 チ チ		
to	止 止 と	me	女 め め
to	止 止 ト	me	女 女 メ
ni	二 二 二	wa	和 和 わ
fu	不 ふ ふ	wa	和 和 ワ
fu	不 ネ フ		

Sample Kanji Chart

A sample from the kanji charts is explained below.

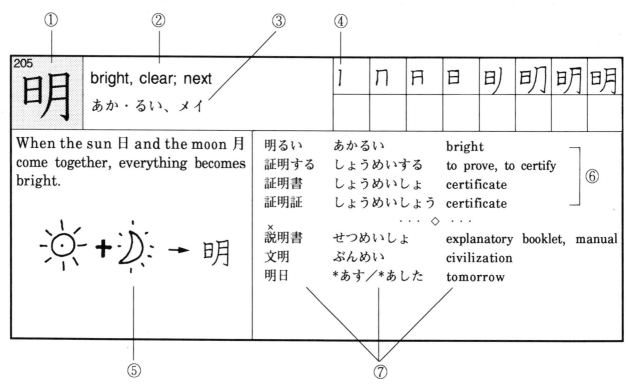

① The kanji and its serial number in this textbook.
② Meanings.
③ Readings: *kun*-readings in hiragana, and *on*-readings in katakana.
Hiragana following a dot [・るい in the sample above] are *okurigana*.
Readings in parentheses ( ) express euphonic change, i.e., modified readings [e.g., ヒャク、(ビャク) in kanji 11 百].
④ Stroke order.
⑤ Etymology or memory-aid. (The authors have created new derivations for some kanji when the etymology is unclear or confusing.)
⑥ Important compound words, and their readings and meanings.
⑦ Additional compound words, and their readings and meanings.

Note: 1) Kanji marked ˣ are not included in the 250 kanji taught in this textbook.
2) Kana in parentheses ( ) in kanji compounds is optional when writing [e.g., 終(わ)る can be written 終わる or 終る]. Two sets of ( ) appears for most nouns derived from compound verbs. The kana in both ( ) or in the former ( ) only may be omitted, but the kana in the latter ( ) alone cannot be omitted [e.g., 取(り)消(し) can be written 取り消し, 取消し, or 取消, but not 取り消].
3) * indicates exceptional readings.
4) Small numbers placed above certain kanji in the Vocabulary sections refer to Lesson numbers.

THE LESSONS

なにか たべましょう

As IN many other countries, eating out in Japan is a popular alternative to cooking at home. There are a variety of restaurants, with the most popular being *soba-ya* (*soba* shops), *shokudō* (inexpensive eateries), and *famirii resutoran* (family restaurants). In most *shokudō* one can order simple Japanese, Western, or Chinese meals. Plastic models of some of the dishes are usually displayed with prices in an outside showcase, as shown in the above picture. In this lesson you will learn how to write numerals in kanji, since this is how they are written in restaurant menus, newspapers, books written vertically, and various other documents.

1 INTRODUCTORY QUIZ

Look at the illustration below, and refer to the words in VOCABULARY. Then try the following quiz.

In a *shokudō*, you will often find the names and prices of dishes written on paper and hung on the wall. Write the correct answers in the spaces provided below.

Ex. わたしは　そばを　たべました。＿＿480＿＿円でした。

1. プレムさんは　うどんを　たべました。＿四百七十＿＿＿＿円でした。

2. リーさんは　カレーライスを　たべて、コーヒーを　のみました。
＿九百三十＿＿＿＿円でした。

3. ラーメンは　＿＿五百＿＿＿＿円です。

4. しょくどうの　でんわばんごうは　＿三九〇二の五七九一＿です。

5. あなたは　この　しょくどうで　なにを　たべますか。
＿＿ラーメン＿＿＿＿を　たべます。

6. いくらですか。
＿＿五百＿＿＿＿円です。

2 VOCABULARY

Study the readings and meanings of these words to help you understand the INTRODUCTORY QUIZ.

1. そば		buckwheat noodles
2. 四百八十円	よん ひゃく はち じゅう えん	480 yen
3. うどん		Japanese noodles
4. 四百七十円	よん ひゃく なな じゅう えん	470 yen
5. カレーライス		curry and rice
6. 六百三十円	ろっ ぴゃく さん じゅう えん	630 yen
7. コーヒー		coffee
8. 三百円	さん びゃく えん	300 yen
9. ラーメン		ramen
10. 五百円	ご ひゃく えん	500 yen
11. でんわばんごう		phone number
12. 三九〇二 – 五七九一	さん きゅう れい に　ご なな きゅう いち	3902-5791

3 NEW CHARACTERS

Twelve characters are introduced in this lesson. Use the explanations to help you understand and remember the characters. Study the compound words to increase your vocabulary.

一　二　三　四　五　六　七　八　九　十　百　円

1 一	one ひと・つ、イチ、（イッ）		一							

一 derives from a pictograph of one finger.	一つ	ひとつ	one
	一	いち	one
		· · · ◇ · · ·	
	一人	ひとり	one person
	一円	いちえん	one yen
	一日	いちにち	a day; all day
	一本	いっぽん	one slender object
	一日	*ついたち	the first (date)

一 derives from a pictograph of one finger.

23

2 二	two ふた・つ、ニ	一	二						

二 derives from a pictograph of two fingers.

二つ	ふたつ	two
二	に	two
	・・・◇・・・	
二人	ふたり	two people
二月	にがつ	February
二日	*ふつか	the second (date); (for) two days

3 三	three みっ・つ、サン	一	二	三					

三 derives from a pictograph of three fingers.

三つ	みっつ	three
三	さん	three
	・・・◇・・・	
三日	みっか	the third (date); (for) three days
三月	さんがつ	March
三人	さんにん	three people

4 四	four よっ・つ、よん、よ、シ	丨	冂	冂	四	四			

四 derives from a pictograph of four fingers.

四つ	よっつ	four
四	よん	four
四	し	four
	・・・◇・・・	
四日	よっか	the fourth (date); (for) four days
四百	よんひゃく	four hundred
四円	よえん	four yen
四時	よじ	four o'clock
四月	しがつ	April

5 五	five いつ・つ、ゴ	一	丁	万	五				

五 is 二 plus 三, meaning five.

五つ	いつつ	five
五	ご	five
		・・・◇・・・
五日	いつか	the fifth (date); (for) five days
五月	ごがつ	May
五十	ごじゅう	fifty

6 六	six むっ・つ、ロク、（ロッ）	，	二	亠	六				

六 derives from a pictograph of a hand showing the number six in the Chinese way of counting on one's fingers.

六つ	むっつ	six
六	ろく	six
		・・・◇・・・
六月	ろくがつ	June
六十	ろくじゅう	sixty
六分	ろっぷん	six minutes
六日	*むいか	the sixth (date); (for) six days

7 七	seven なな・つ、なな、シチ	一	七						

七 depicts two fingers on five fingers, meaning seven.

七つ	ななつ	seven
七	なな	seven
七	しち	seven
		・・・◇・・・
七百	ななひゃく	seven hundred
七月	しちがつ	July
七時	しちじ	seven o'clock
七日	*なのか	the seventh (date); (for) seven days

8 八 — eight
やっ・つ、ハチ、（ハッ）

筆順: ノ 八

八 derives from a pictograph of two hands, each showing four fingers, meaning eight. When 八 is used as part of other kanji, it often means divide because of its shape.

八つ	やっつ	eight
八	はち	eight
… ◇ …		
八月	はちがつ	August
八百	はっぴゃく	eight hundred
八日	*ようか	the eighth (date); (for) eight days

9 九 — nine
ここの・つ、キュウ、ク

筆順: ノ 九

九 depicts an arm with tightened muscles and is used to mean nine, the number that tightens up and completes the series of single digits.

九つ	ここのつ	nine
九	きゅう	nine
九	く	nine
… ◇ …		
九日	ここのか	the ninth (date); (for) nine days
九十	きゅうじゅう	ninety
九州	きゅうしゅう	Kyushu (island, district)
九月	くがつ	September
九時	くじ	nine o'clock

10 十 — ten
とお、ジュウ、（ジッ／ジュッ）

筆順: 一 十

十 derives from a pictograph of two crossing hands with ten fingers. When used as part of other kanji, 十 often means add (e.g., 184 協, 204 博, 219 計, 239 汁).

十	とお	ten
十	じゅう	ten
十一	じゅういち	eleven
三十	さんじゅう	thirty
… ◇ …		
十日	とおか	the tenth (date); (for) ten days
十一円	じゅういちえん	eleven yen
十分	じっぷん／じゅっぷん	ten minutes
二十日	*はつか	the twentieth (date); (for) twenty days

11 百 — hundred

ヒャク、（ビャク）、（ピャク）

一 ア ア 百 百 百

百 combines 一 one and 白 rice grain, and represents one bag of rice. This suggests a large number, at least a hundred. 白 by itself means white, the color of rice.

⊘ → ⊘ → 白

百	ひゃく	one hundred
四百	よんひゃく	four hundred
三百	さんびゃく	three hundred
六百	ろっぴゃく	six hundred
八百	はっぴゃく	eight hundred
· · · ◇ · · ·		
九百円	きゅうひゃくえん	nine hundred yen
何百	なんびゃく	how many hundreds; hundreds of ~

12 円 — circle; yen

エン

丨 冂 冂 円

円 derives from 圓, which combines 囗 encircle, 口 mouth or man (cf. 107), and 貝 money (cf. 200 費). Originally indicating encircled things, 円 then came to mean circle, round, and, as an associated meaning, yen, because yen coins are round.

円	えん	yen; circle
十円	じゅうえん	ten yen
五十円	ごじゅうえん	fifty yen
百円	ひゃくえん	one hundred yen
七百円	ななひゃくえん	seven hundred yen
· · · ◇ · · ·		
円高	えんだか	high value of the yen
円安	えんやす	low value of the yen

4 PRACTICE

I. Write the readings of the following kanji in hiragana.

1. 一　　　2. 二　　　3. 三　　　4. 四　　　5. 五　　　6. 六

い、イチ、ひとつ　　ニ、ふたつ　　サン、みっつ　　シ、よ、よん、よっつ　　ゴ、いつつ　　ロク、むっつ

7. 七　　　8. 八　　　9. 九　　10. 十　　11. 四十　　12. 九十

シチ、ななつ、なな　　ハチ、やっつ　　ク、キュウ、ここのつ　　ジュウ、とお　　よんじゅう　　きゅうじゅう

13. 二十九円　　　　14. 七十四円　　　　15. 九十七円

にじゅうくえん　　　　ななじゅうよんえん　　　　きゅうじゅうななえん

16. 百　　　17. 二百　　18. 三百　　19. 四百　　20. 五百

ひゃく　　　にひゃく　　さんびゃく　　よんひゃく　　ごひゃく

21. 六百　　22. 七百　　23. 八百　　24. 九百

ろっぴゃく　　ななひゃく　　はっぴゃく　　きゅうひゃく

25. 五 つ　　26. 三 つ　　27. 六 つ　　28. 二 つ　　29. 八 つ
いつつ　　　　みっつ　　　　むっつ　　　　ふたつ　　　　やっつ

30. 四 つ　　31. 九 つ　　32. 十　　　33. 一 つ　　34. 七 つ
よっつ　　　ここのつ　　　　とう　　　　ひとつ　　　　ななつ

35. 三 百 十 一 円
さんびゃくじゅういちえん

36. わたしの　でんわばんごうは　〇三　－　五二七六　－　四一九八です。
　　　　　　　　　　　　　　れいさんの　ごにしちろく　の　よんいちくはち
　　　　　　　　　　　　　　03-5276-4198

Ⅱ. Fill in the blanks with appropriate kanji.

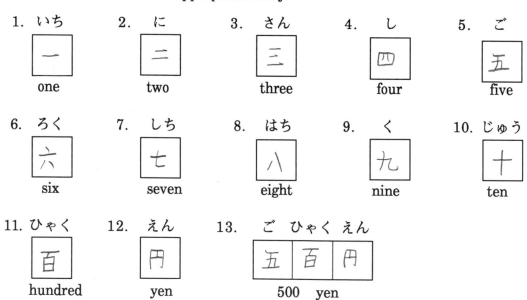

1. いち　　2. に　　　3. さん　　4. し　　　5. ご
一　　　　二　　　　三　　　　四　　　　五
one　　　two　　　three　　　four　　　five

6. ろく　　7. しち　　8. はち　　9. く　　　10. じゅう
六　　　　七　　　　八　　　　九　　　　十
six　　　seven　　　eight　　　nine　　　ten

11. ひゃく　　12. えん　　13. ご ひゃく えん
百　　　　　　円　　　　　　五　百　円
hundred　　　yen　　　　　500　yen

スキーに いきます

SKIING HAS become an increasingly popular winter sport in Japan. Many skiers take advantage of ski buses, which travel between large cities and ski areas during the winter. The fares are reasonable and the buses usually leave the city late in the evening and arrive at the slopes early the next morning. In this lesson, you will learn kanji for dates, time, and some travel-related words.

1 INTRODUCTORY QUIZ

Look at the illustration below and refer to the words in VOCABULARY. Then try the following quiz.

Below left is a memo belonging to a student who plans to go skiing during the winter vacation. Below right is part of a ski bus brochure. At any travel agency, information is available about ski buses bound for famous ski areas, some of which are located in hot-spring resorts, such as Zao Onsen.

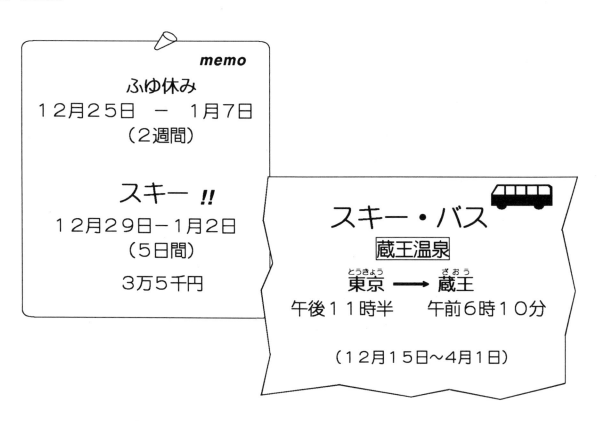

I. Choose the correct answers.

1. スキーは　いつからですか。

    a. 12日29月   b. 12日29日   c. 12月29日

2. スキーは　なんにちまでですか。

    a. ついたち   b. ふつか   c. みっか

3. なんにちかん、スキーに　いきますか。

    a. よっかかん   b. いつかかん   c. むいかかん

4. スキー・バスは　なんじに　東京を　*でますか。   (*start)

    a. 11:00 p.m.   b. 11:30 p.m.   c. 11:30 a.m.

5. スキー・バスは　なんじに　蔵王に　*つきますか。   (*arrive)

    a. 6:10 p.m.   b. 6:10 a.m.   c. 6:00 a.m.

6. バスに　なんじかん　のりますか。
　　　a. 6時間半　　　　b. 6時間40分　　　c. 7時間

7. スキーの　*ひようは　いくらですか。　　　　　　　　　(*cost)
　　　a. ¥350　　　　　b. ¥3,500　　　　c. ¥35,000

Ⅱ. Fill in the spaces provided with hiragana and Arabic numerals.

1. ふゆやすみは　いつからですか。
　　_____からです。

2. ふゆやすみは　いつまでですか。
　　_____までです。

3. ふゆやすみは　*どのくらい　ありますか。　　　　　　(*how long)
　　_____あります。

4. スキー・バスは　いつから　いつまで　ありますか。
　　_____から　_____まで　あります。

2 VOCABULARY

Study the readings and meanings of these words to help you understand the INTRODUCTORY QUIZ.

1. 12月29日	じゅう に がつ に じゅう く にち	December 29
2. なん日	なん にち	what day
3. 一日	ついたち	the 1st (date)
4. 二日	ふつ か	the 2nd (date)
5. 三日	みっ か	the 3rd (date)
6. 1月2日	いち がつ ふつ か	January 2
7. なん日間	なん にち かん	how many days
8. 四日間	よっ か かん	(for) 4 days
9. 五日間	いつ か かん	(for) 5 days
10. 六日間	むい か かん	(for) 6 days
11. スキー・バス		bus headed for ski slopes
12. なん時	なん じ	what time
13. 蔵王温泉	ざ おう おん せん	Zao Onsen (hot-spring resort)
14. 東京	とう きょう	Tokyo
15. 蔵王	ざ おう	Zao (place)

16. 午後	ご ご	(in the) afternoon
17. 11時半	じゅう いち じ はん	11:30
18. 午前	ご ぜん	(in the) morning
19. 6時10分	ろく じ じっ／じゅっ ぷん	6:10
20. なん時間	なん じ かん	how many hours
21. 6時間半	ろく じ かん はん	6 and 1/2 hours
22. 6時間40分	ろく じ かん よん じっ／じゅっ ぷん	6 hours and 40 minutes
23. 3万5千円	さん まん ご せん えん	35,000 yen
24. ふゆ休み	ふゆ やすみ	winter vacation
25. 12月25日	じゅう に がつ に じゅう ご にち	December 25
26. 1月7日	いち がつ なの か	January 7
27. 2週間	に しゅう かん	(for) 2 weeks
28. 12月15日	じゅう に がつ じゅう ご にち	December 15
29. 4月1日	し がつ ついたち	April 1

3 NEW CHARACTERS

Thirteen characters are introduced in this lesson. Use the explanations to help you understand and remember the characters. Study the compound words to increase your vocabulary.

休 月 日 週 間 千 万 午 前 後 時 半 分

13 休	rest; absence やす・む、キュウ	ノ イ イ- イ- イ木 休

休, which combines the radical イ man (cf. 102 人) and 木 tree (cf. 29), represents a man taking a rest under a tree.

彳 → 人 → イ

→ 休

休む	やすむ	to be absent; to rest
休み	やすみ	vacation, holiday; break; absence

· · · ◇ · · ·

冬休み	ふゆやすみ	winter vacation
夏休み	なつやすみ	summer vacation
休学する	きゅうがくする	to take time off from school

14 月 — moon; month
つき、ゲツ、ガツ、（ガッ）

）	刀	月	月				

月 derives from a pictograph of the moon. Month is an associated meaning, since the moon waxes and wanes once a month.

月	つき	moon, month
四か月	よんかげつ	(for) four months
一月	いちがつ	January
十二月	じゅうにがつ	December
	・・・◇・・・	
月曜日	げつようび	Monday
今月	こんげつ	this month
何月	なんがつ	which month
生年月日	せいねんがっぴ	date of birth

15 日 — sun; day
ひ、び、か、ニチ、ジツ

）	冂	日	日				

日 derives from an ancient Chinese pictograph of the sun. 日 also means day, because the sun rises and sets every day.

日	ひ	day
二日	ふつか	the second (date); (for) two days
一日	いちにち	a day; all day
休日	きゅうじつ	holiday, day off
一日	*ついたち	the first (date)
	・・・◇・・・	
日曜日	にちようび	Sunday
今日	こんにち	nowadays
今日	*きょう	today

16 週 — week
シュウ

）	刀	月	用	用	用	周	周
｀周	冯	週					

週 combines 周, paddy with rice from a basket scattered all around, and the radical 辶, meaning proceed or road. Thus 週 suggests the time, perhaps a week, required to go all around a paddy to look after it.

週	しゅう	week
	・・・◇・・・	
毎週	まいしゅう	every week
今週	こんしゅう	this week
先週	せんしゅう	last week
来週	らいしゅう	next week
週末	しゅうまつ	weekend

33

17 間	between; interval, while; room, space あいだ、ま、カン、（ゲン）	丨 冂 冂 冃 冂' 門 門 門 門 門 門 間

間 depicts the sun 日 between the doors of a gate 門 (cf. 181). Associated meanings are interval, while, room, and space.

間	あいだ	between; interval
二週間	にしゅうかん	(for) two weeks
五日間	いつかかん	(for) five days
	・・・◇・・・	
この間	このあいだ	the other day
日本間	にほんま	Japanese-style room
何週間	なんしゅうかん	how many weeks
何日間	なんにちかん	how many days
人間	にんげん	human being

---

18 千	thousand ち、セン、（ゼン）	ノ 二 千

千, which combines 十 ten and 亻 man (cf. 102 人), formerly meant many people and eventually came to mean thousand.

二千	にせん	two thousand
千円	せんえん	one thousand yen
五千円	ごせんえん	five thousand yen
三千	さんぜん	three thousand
	・・・◇・・・	
千葉	ちば	Chiba (place)

---

19 万	ten thousand マン、バン	一 万 万

万 derives from an ancient Indian religious symbol 卐, which changed into 卍 later in China, meaning ten thousand gods.

二万円	にまんえん	twenty thousand yen
百万円	ひゃくまんえん	one million yen
	・・・◇・・・	
万国	ばんこく	all nations

20 午	noon ゴ	ノ ⊢ 午 午					

午 depicts a pestle used for pounding rice. The up-and-down motion of the pestle suggests the turning of morning to afternoon, namely, noon.

		··· ◇ ···
正午	しょうご	noon

21 前	front, before, earlier まえ、ゼン	丶 丷 ⺍ 亠 亣 亓 亓 前

前 combines 止 foot (cf. 150 止 stop) on a boat, suggesting a boat that cannot move, and 刂 sword. The sword is used to cut the boat's rope, allowing it to go forward. Thus 前 means front. Associated meanings are before and earlier.

前	まえ	the front
午前	ごぜん	(in the) morning
前日	ぜんじつ	the previous day, the day before
		··· ◇ ···
五分前	ごふんまえ	five minutes before / ago
三日前	みっかまえ	three days before / ago

22 後	behind, back, after, later あと、うし・ろ、ゴ、コウ	ノ ク 彳 彳 彳 往 往 後

後, which combines 彳 go (cf. 104 行), 幺 weak ply, and 夂 trailing leg, suggests walking while dragging a weak leg and falling behind. Thus 後 means behind or after.

後	あと	the back; the rest; afterwards
前後	ぜんご	before and after, before and behind
午後	ごご	(in the) afternoon
		··· ◇ ···
後ろ	うしろ	the back, the rear
後半	こうはん	the latter half

23 時 — time; hour / とき、ジ

Stroke order: 丨 冂 冃 日 日⁻ 日⁺ 旷 昨 時 時

時 combines 日 sun and 寺 foot and hand, suggesting move or work. As the sun moves, time goes by. 寺 by itself means temple, a place where priests work.

時	とき	time, hour
六時	ろくじ	six o'clock
時間	じかん	time, hour
日時	にちじ	the date and time
· · · ◇ · · ·		
時々	ときどき	sometimes, once in a while
何時間	なんじかん	how many hours
時計	*とけい	watch, clock

(Note: 々 is used in place of the latter of two successive identical kanji.)

24 半 — half / ハン、(パン)

Stroke order: 丶 丷 丷 半 半

半 depicts a vertical line dividing (cf. 8 八) a board into two halves.

十一時半	じゅういちじ はん	half past eleven
半日	はんにち	half a day
· · · ◇ · · ·		
半年	はんとし	half a year
前半	ぜんはん/ぜんぱん	the first half

25 分 — divide, portion; minute; understand / わ・かる、わ・ける、ブン、フン、(プン)

Stroke order: 丿 八 分 分

分, which combines 八 divide (cf. 8) and 刀 knife, means divide or portion. One hour is divided into sixty minutes. Dividing a question into solvable pieces suggests understanding.

分(か)る	わかる	to understand
分ける	わける	to divide, to separate
半分	はんぶん	half
九分	きゅうふん	nine minutes
四分	よんぷん	four minutes
· · · ◇ · · ·		
三日分	みっかぶん	three days' worth

4 PRACTICE

I. How to Read Time

MINUTES

1 — 一分　いっぷん
2 — 二分　にふん
3 — 三分　さんぷん
4 — 四分　よんぷん
5 — 五分　ごふん
6 — 六分　ろっぷん
7 — 七分　ななふん
8 — 八分　はちふん/はっぷん
9 — 九分　きゅうふん
10 — 十分　じっぷん/じゅっぷん
11 — 十一分　じゅういっぷん
12 — 十二分　じゅうにふん
13 — 十三分　じゅうさんぷん
14 — 十四分　じゅうよんぷん
15 — 十五分　じゅうごふん

HOURS

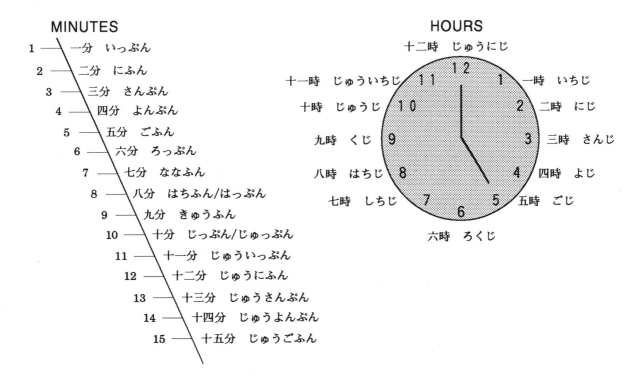

十二時　じゅうにじ
十一時　じゅういちじ
十時　じゅうじ
九時　くじ
八時　はちじ
七時　しちじ
一時　いちじ
二時　にじ
三時　さんじ
四時　よじ
五時　ごじ
六時　ろくじ

三時二十分　さんじ に じっ/じゅっ ぷん

十時半　じゅう じ はん

七時十分前　しち じ じっ/じゅっ ぷん まえ

II. Write the readings of the follwing kanji in hiragana.

1. 十二月　　　2. 二十九日　　3. 一月一日　　4. 二日

5. 三日　　　　6. 四日間　　　7. 五日間　　　8. 六日間

9. 午後　　　10. 十一時半　11. 午前　　　12. 六時十分

13. 三万円　　14. 五千円　　15. 七日　　　16. 二月

17. 三月　　　18. 四月　　　19. 五月　　　20. 六月

21. 七月　　　22. 八月　　　23. 九月　　　24. 十月

25. 十一月　　26. 一か月　　27. 四か月　　28. 六か月

29. 九 か 月　　30. 八 日　　31. 九 日　　32. 十 日

33. 十 九 日　　34. 二 十 日　　35. 千　　36. 三 千

37. 四 千　　38. 八 千　　39. 九 千　　40. 四 万

41. 九 万　　42. 四 時　　43. 一 分　　44. 四 分

45. 六 分　　46. 七 分　　47. 八 分　　48. 九 分

49. なつ休みは　なん日間ですか。　十四日間、二週間です。

50. けさ　なん時に　おきましたか。　九時です。

51. バスに　なん時間　のりますか。　六時間半　のります。

Ⅲ. Fill in the blanks with appropriate kanji.

1. やす
□ む
to rest

2. きゅう じつ
□□
day off

3. 　　ひ
ははの □
Mother's Day

4. 　　にち
十三 □
the 13th (date)

5. 　か
七 □
the 7th (date)

6. 　げつ
四か □
for 4 months

7. 　がつ
十 □
October

8. せん
□ 円
1,000 yen

9. ぜん
三 □ 円
3,000 yen

10. まん
百 □ 円
1,000,000 yen

11. しゅう かん
一 □□
for 1 week

12. まえ　　あと
□ と □
before and after

13. ご ぜん
□□
in the morning

14. ご ご
□□
in the afternoon

15. とき
□
time

16. じ　　ふん
八 □ 五 □
8:05

17. ぷん
三 □
3 minutes

18. はん ぶん
□□
half

きょうは なん曜日ですか

IN ADDITION to using the Western system for counting years, a traditional system based on the reign of the emperors is used in Japan. Thus the year 1993 is also referred to as Heisei 5. There are 14 national holidays a year in Japan. One long series of holidays that goes from the end of April to the beginning of May is known as Golden Week. Golden Week ends with Children's Day on May 5, during which parents with boys fly carp banners above their homes. This expresses their wish that their children grow up strong and healthy like carps. In this lesson, you will learn kanji used in calendars and other time-related words.

1 INTRODUCTORY QUIZ

Look at the calendar below and refer to the words in VOCABULARY. Then try the following quiz.

Saturdays and Sundays are holidays for most government offices, post offices, banks, and many companies. When a national holiday falls on a Sunday, the following Monday automatically becomes a holiday. Fill in the spaces provided with hiragana and Arabic numerals.

```
          五月

平成五年              1 9 9 3
    _____
    日   月   火   水   木   金   土
                                1
    2   ③   ④   ⑤   6   7   8
    9   10  11  12  13  14  15
    16  17  18  19  20  21  22
    23  24  25  26  27  28  29
    30  31
```

○祝日 (祭日)

③ 5月3日　けんぽう きねん日　　Constitution Day
④ 5月4日　こくみんの 休日　　　national holiday
⑤ 5月5日　こどもの 日　　　　　Children's Day

1. これは ＿＿＿＿＿＿五年 (1993) の　カレンダーです。

2. 五月の　祝日 (祭日) は　みっかと ＿＿＿＿＿＿と ＿＿＿＿＿＿です。

3. それは ＿＿＿＿曜日と ＿＿＿＿曜日と ＿＿＿＿曜日です。

4. 五月には、もく曜日が ＿＿＿＿* かい　あります。　　　　　　(*times)

5. にち曜日が ＿＿＿＿かい　あります。

6. 五月十四日は ＿＿＿＿曜日です。

7. 五月二十九日は ＿＿＿＿曜日です。

8. 五月の　休日は ＿＿＿＿かい　あります。

9. 平日は ＿＿＿＿曜日から ＿＿＿＿曜日までです。

2 VOCABULARY

Study the readings and meanings of these words to help you understand the INTRODUCTORY QUIZ.

1. 平成	へい せい	Heisei (era)
2. 五年	ご ねん	the 5th year
3. 祝日	しゅく じつ	national holiday
4. 祭日	さい じつ	national holiday (used interchangeably with しゅく じつ)
5. 日曜日	にち よう び	Sunday
6. 月曜日	げつ よう び	Monday
7. 火曜日	か よう び	Tuesday
8. 水曜日	すい よう び	Wednesday
9. 木曜日	もく よう び	Thursday
10. 金曜日	きん よう び	Friday
11. 土曜日	ど よう び	Saturday
12. 休日	きゅう じつ	holiday, day off
13. 平日	へい じつ	ordinary day, weekday

3 NEW CHARACTERS

Eleven characters are introduced in this lesson. Use the explanations to help you understand and remember the characters. Study the compound words to increase your vocabulary.

曜 火 水 木 金 土 平 成 年 祝 祭

26 曜

day of the week

ヨウ

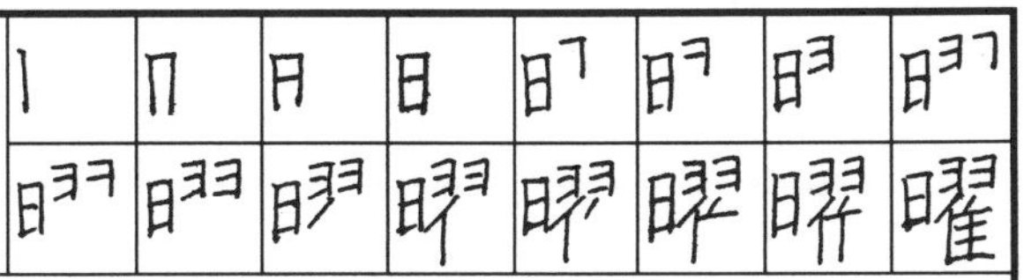

曜 combines 日 sun, ヨヨ wings, and 隹 fat bird. The sun flying on a bird's wings suggests a day of the week.

日曜日	にちようび	Sunday
月曜日	げつようび	Monday
	. . . ◇ . . .	
何曜日	なんようび／なにようび	what day of the week

27 火 — fire, flame
ひ、（び）、カ

丶	丶ノ	少	火			

火 derives from a pictograph of a flame. When used as the lower part of other kanji, 火 is sometimes written 灬.

火	ひ	fire, flame
火曜日	かようび	Tuesday

· · · ◇ · · ·

×花火	はなび	fireworks
火事	かじ	fire (destructive burning)

---

28 水 — water
みず、スイ

亅	刀	水	水			

水, modified from 川 river, means water. As a radical, 水 is often written 氵.

水	みず	water
水曜日	すいようび	Wednesday

· · · ◇ · · ·

×御茶ノ水	おちゃのみず	Ochanomizu (place)
×冷水	れいすい	ice water, cold water
水分	すいぶん	moisture

---

29 木 — tree, wood
き、（ぎ）、ボク、モク

一	十	才	木			

木 derives from a pictograph of a tree.

木	き	tree, wood
木曜日	もくようび	Thursday

· · · ◇ · · ·

六本木	ろっぽんぎ	Roppongi (place)
土木	どぼく	abbreviation for 土木工事 (public works) and 土木工学 (civil engineering)
木×造	もくぞう	wooden, made of wood

30 金	gold, metal; money かね、キン	ノ	入	人	今	全	全	余	金

金, which depicts two nuggets in the earth 土 (cf. 31) piled up in a mound ᐱ, indicates precious ore such as gold. Associated meanings are metal and money.

金	かね	money / metal
金	きん	gold
金曜日	きんようび	Friday

· · · ◇ · · ·

金メダル	きんメダル	gold medal
現金	げんきん	cash
礼金	れいきん	gift money to landlord

---

31 土	soil, earth; ground つち、ド、ト	一	十	土					

土 represents a plant growing out of the earth, suggesting soil or ground.

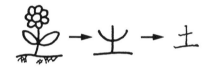

土	つち	soil, earth
土曜日	どようび	Saturday

· · · ◇ · · ·

| 土地 | とち | (piece of) land |

---

32 平	flat, level たい・ら、ヘイ	一	一	五	立	平			

平 represents a waterweed floating flat on the water.

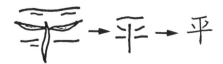

平日	へいじつ	ordinary day, weekday

· · · ◇ · · ·

平らな	たいらな	flat
水平な	すいへいな	horizontal, level
平均する	へいきんする	to average

33 成	achieve; become, form な・る、セイ	ノ	厂	万	成	成	成		

成, which combines 戈 arms or weapon and 力 power or force (cf. 67 男), means achieve. Associated meanings are form and become.

平成	へいせい	Heisei (era)
· · · ◇ · · ·		
成田	なりた	Narita (place, airport)
成績表	せいせきひょう	school report card
成人の日	せいじんのひ	Coming of Age Day
成功する	せいこうする	to succeed, to be successful

34 年	year; age とし、ネン	ノ	ト	仁	午	左	年		

年 depicts a man working in a rice paddy (cf. 102 人) and grain. This suggests the period between harvests, which is usually a year.

年	とし	year; age
三年	さんねん	three years, the third year
· · · ◇ · · ·		
今年	ことし	this year
去年	きょねん	last year
年度	ねんど	fiscal / academic year
年金	ねんきん	pension
忘年会	ぼうねんかい	year-end party

35 祝	celebrate, congratulate いわ・う、シュク	丶	ラ	オ	ネ	ネ	初	初	祝
		祝							

祝 combines 礻 and 兄. The radical 礻 derives from 示 altar, and 兄 represents a kneeling priest. Thus 祝 means celebration. 兄 by itself means elder brother.

祝う	いわう	to celebrate, to congratulate
(お)祝い	(お)いわい	congratulation, celebratory gift
祝日	しゅくじつ	national holiday, festival day
· · · ◇ · · ·		
内祝(い)	うちいわい	family celebration
祝電	しゅくでん	congratulatory telegram

36 祭	festival まつ・り、サイ	

祭 derives from a pictograph of a hand 又 (cf. 88 手) holding sacrificial meat 月 (cf. 226 肉) on an altar 示 (cf. 35 祝). Thus 祭 suggests an occasion when offerings are made to the gods; i.e., a festival.		
祭(り)	まつり	festival
祭日	さいじつ	festival day, national holiday
祝祭日	しゅくさいじつ	national holiday, festival day
	・・・ ◇ ・・・	
大学祭	だいがくさい	university / college festival

4 PRACTICE

Ⅰ. Write the readings of the following kanji in hiragana.

1. 平 成 五 年　2. 祝 日　3. 祭 日　4. 日 曜 日　5. 月 曜 日

6. 火 曜 日　7. 水 曜 日　8. 木 曜 日　9. 金 曜 日　10. 土 曜 日

11. 休 日　12. 平 日　13. 祝 う　14. 祭 り

15. 火は　あかいです。

16. この　水は　おいしいですね。

17. 五月は　木が　きれいです。

18. お金は　かばんの　なかに　あります。

19. 1992年は、オリンピックの　年でした。

Ⅱ. Fill in the blanks with appropriate kanji.

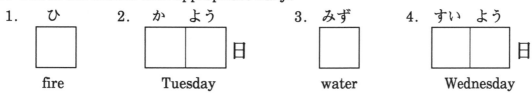

1. ひ □ fire　2. か よう □□日 Tuesday　3. みず □ water　4. すい よう □□日 Wednesday

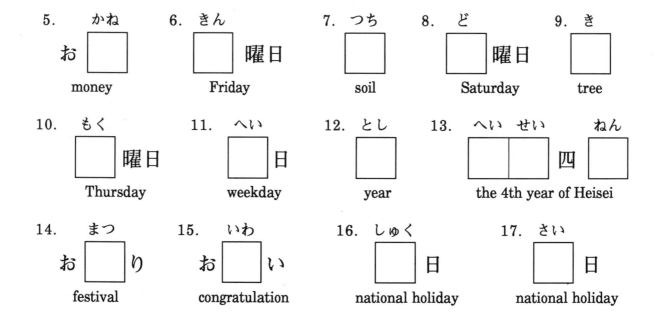

5. かね
お[ ]
money

6. きん
[ ]曜日
Friday

7. つち
[ ]
soil

8. ど
[ ]曜日
Saturday

9. き
[ ]
tree

10. もく
[ ]曜日
Thursday

11. へい
[ ]日
weekday

12. とし
[ ]
year

13. へい せい　ねん
[ ][ ]四[ ]
the 4th year of Heisei

14. まつ
お[ ]り
festival

15. いわ
お[ ]い
congratulation

16. しゅく
[ ]日
national holiday

17. さい
[ ]日
national holiday

はじめまして、どうぞ よろしく

THE ACADEMIC year in Japan begins in April. An entrance ceremony is held for incoming university freshmen, and the president and deans give welcome addresses. When classes begin, new students are often asked to introduce themselves. This lesson will help you introduce yourself in Japanese.

The photo to the right shows a street address. These address signs are often attached to buildings or utility poles, and are helpful if you are looking for a particular place.

1 INTRODUCTORY QUIZ

Look at the illustration below and refer to the words in VOCABULARY. Then try the following quiz.

文京区
本郷七丁目3

はじめまして、わたしは　リーです。
マレーシアの　留学生です。四月から
東京大学の　工学部で　べんきょう
します。　専攻は　土木工学です。
わたしの　先生は　三木先生です。
日本語も　べんきょうします。
都市工学科に　ともだちが　います。
あしたは　入学式です。

Mr. Lee, a student from Malaysia, is planning to study civil engineering in the Faculty of Engineering at the University of Tokyo; he will study Japanese, too. The entrance ceremony will be held tomorrow. Read the following sentences and choose the correct answers.

1. わたしは　リーです。（ a. とうきょう　　b. きょうと ）大学の　がくせいです。

2. （ a. こうがくぶ　　b. ぶんがくぶ ）の　（ a. とし　　b. どぼく ）工学科で　べんきょう　します。

3. わたしの　せんこうは　（ a. 日本語　　b. 土木工学 ）です。

4. （ a. 学生　　b. 先生 ）の　なまえは　三木せんせいです。

5. 大学の　にゅうがくしきは　（ a. 四月　　b. 八月 ）です。

6. 東京大学は　（ a. 左京区　　b. 文京区 ）、本郷（ a. 七丁目　　b. 七十日 ）に　あります。

2 VOCABULARY

Study the readings and meanings of these words to help you understand the INTRODUCTORY QUIZ.

1.	東京大学	とう きょう だい がく	University of Tokyo
2.	京都大学	きょう と だい がく	Kyoto University
3.	学生	がく せい	student
4.	留学生	りゅう がく せい	foreign student
5.	工学部	こう がく ぶ	Faculty of Engineering
6.	文学部	ぶん がく ぶ	Faculty of Literature
7.	都市工学科	と し こう がっ か	Department of Urban Engineering
8.	土木工学科	ど ぼく こう がっ か	Department of Civil Engineering
9.	専攻	せん こう	major field of study
10.	日本語	に ほん ご	Japanese language
11.	先生	せん せい	professor, teacher
12.	三木	み き	Miki (name)
13.	入学式	にゅう がく しき	entrance ceremony
14.	左京区	さ きょう く	Sakyo Ward
15.	文京区	ぶん きょう く	Bunkyo Ward
16.	本郷	ほん ごう	Hongo (place)
17.	七丁目	なな ちょう め	the 7th block (in an address)

3 NEW CHARACTERS

Twenty-two characters are introduced in this lesson. Use the explanations to help you understand and remember the characters. Study the compound words to increase your vocabulary.

大 学 東 京 留 生 工 部 科 専 攻 先 本 語 都
市 入 式 文 区 丁 目

---

37 大 big, large, great
おお・きい、ダイ、タイ

一 ナ 大

大 depicts a man with arms and legs spread wide, suggesting big and large.

大きい	おおきい	big, large, great, tall
		・・・◇・・・
大阪	おおさか	Osaka
大都市	だいとし	big city
大仏	だいぶつ	great statue of Buddha
大会	たいかい	large meeting, convention; tournament

---

38 学 study, learn; school
まな・ぶ、ガク、（ガッ）

、 ⺍ ⺍ ⺍ 兴 学 学 学

学, simplified from 學, combines 子 child (cf. 117) and ⺍, which represents a building with lights on in the kanji 営 (cf. 90). Thus 学 indicates a building where children are, namely, a school. An associated meaning is study.

大学	だいがく	university, college
学年	がくねん	school / academic year; grade at school
		・・・◇・・・
学ぶ	まなぶ	to study, to learn
学校	がっこう	school

| 39 東 | east ひがし、トウ | 一 丆 丙 丙 亩 車 東 東 |

東, which combines 木 tree and 日 sun, depicts the sun rising from behind a tree in the east.

東	ひがし	east
東大	とうだい	abbreviation for 東京大学 (University of Tokyo)
	···◇···	
JR東日本	JRひがしにほん	East Japan Railway Company
関東	かんとう	Kanto (district)

| 40 京 | capital キョウ | ` 一 亠 古 古 亨 京 京 |

京 represents a big building on a hill, a sight often seen in a capital city. It also represents stone lanterns that guarded ancient Chinese capitals.

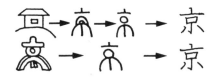

東京	とうきょう	Tokyo
	···◇···	
左京区	さきょうく	Sakyo Ward (in Kyoto)

| 41 留 | stay, keep; fasten と・める、リュウ | ノ ㇉ ㄙ 幻 幻 邠 留 留
 留 留 |

 was originally written 丣, depicting closed doors. 田 means rice paddy (cf. 87), which can be thought of as limited space. Closed doors combined with limited space suggest staying or keeping something in a certain place.

留学する	りゅうがくする	to study abroad
	···◇···	
書留	かきとめ	registered mail
国費留学	こくひ りゅうがく	study abroad on a government scholarship
私費留学	しひ りゅうがく	study abroad on one's own expense

42 生 — live, be born, life
い・きる、う・まれる、セイ、（ジョウ）

Stroke order: ノ ー 生 生 生

生 depicts a flower in its prime, ready to give birth to a new life. Thus 生 means life, living, being born, or giving birth.

生まれる	うまれる	to be born
学生	がくせい	student
留学生	りゅうがくせい	foreign student
生年月日	せいねんがっぴ	date of birth

・・・◇・・・

生きる	いきる	to live
大学生	だいがくせい	university / college student
学生課	がくせいか	Student Affairs Section
一年生	いちねんせい	first-year student, freshman
誕生日	たんじょうび	birthday

43 工 — craft, industry
コウ

Stroke order: 一 丁 工

工, representing a carpenter's ruler, means craft or industry. As part of other kanji, it often means straight.

工学	こうがく	engineering
土木工学	どぼく こうがく	civil engineering

・・・◇・・・

工場	こうじょう	factory
工業	こうぎょう	(manufacturing) industry
人工	じんこう	artificial

44 部 — part, section
ブ

Stroke order: 丶 亠 立 立 立 音 音 音 音 部 部

部 combines 音, which derives from 剖 and means cutting something into parts, and β, indicating village (cf. 51 都, 151 郵). Thus 部 formerly meant part of a village, and now has come to mean part or section in general.

工学部	こうがくぶ	Faculty of Engineering
部分	ぶぶん	part, portion

・・・◇・・・

全部	ぜんぶ	all, whole
テニス部	テニスぶ	tennis club
部屋	*へや	room

45 科	department, course; academic subject カ	ノ	ニ	千	禾	禾	禾	科	科
		科							

科 combines the radical 禾 grain and 斗, which derives from the shape of a dipper used to measure volume in ancient China. Formerly meaning measuring and sorting out, 科 now means subject of study or department.

学科	がっか	university / college department
土木工学科	どぼく こうがっか	Department of Civil Engineering
科学	かがく	science

· · · ◇ · · ·

46 専	specialize; exclusive セン	一	厂	厅	百	百	亩	車	専
		専							

専 combines 亩, depicting a tool used to weave one rope from many strands, and 寸 work (cf. 23 時). Thus 専 means working in one specific area or specializing.

| 専門 | せんもん | major field of study, specialty |

· · · ◇ · · ·

| 専門学校 | せんもん がっこう | vocational / professional school |

47 攻	attack コウ	一	丁	エ	エ′	エ″	功	攻	

攻 combines エ straight (cf. 43) and 攵, representing a hand brandishing a whip. Thus 攻 means attacking in a straightforward way. 攵 is often used to indicate that the whole kanji is a verb.

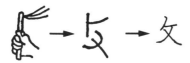

| 専攻する | せんこうする | to specialize / major in |

· · · ◇ · · ·

| 攻撃する | こうげきする | to attack |

48 先	ahead, earlier, previous さき、セン	ノ	ﾉ-	4	生	先	先		

先 combines 生 feet and 儿 legs, the parts of the body that lead a man as he walks. Thus 先 means ahead or previous.

先生	せんせい	teacher, professor
先週	せんしゅう	last week
先月	せんげつ	last month
· · · ◇ · · ·		
連絡先	れんらくさき	where to make contact
先日	せんじつ	the other day
先輩	せんぱい	one's senior

49 本	origin, main; book; counter for long slender objects もと、ホン、（ボン）、（ポン）	一	十	オ	木	本			

Adding a line to the base of 木 tree, 本 means basic, origin, or main. (If the line is added near the top as in 末, it means end or trifle.)

本	ほん	book
日本	にほん/にっぽん	Japan
本部	ほんぶ	head office, headquarters
三本	さんぼん	three slender objects
· · · ◇ · · ·		
山本さん	やまもとさん	Mr./Ms./Miss/Mrs. Yamamoto
本日	ほんじつ	today

50 語	talk, word, language ゴ	、	亠	㝾	言	言	言	言	言
		訂	訪	語	語	語	語		

語 combines 言 speak (cf. 78 話), 五 interact, and 口 mouth (cf. 107). 五 is associated with interact because of its crossing lines. Thus 語 means talk, word, or language.

日本語	にほんご	Japanese language
フランス語	フランスご	French language
· · · ◇ · · ·		
言語	げんご	language
単語	たんご	word, vocabulary
語学	ごがく	language study, linguistics
英語	えいご	English language

51 都	capital, metropolis ト	一 十 土 尹 尹 者 者 者 者 者 都 都 都

都 combines the radical 阝 village and 者, which depicts various foods gathered and cooked on a stove. 都 thus suggests a gathering of many villages, meaning capital city.

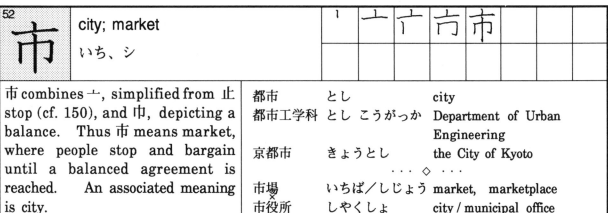

東京都	とうきょうと	Metropolis of Tokyo
京都	きょうと	Kyoto

· · · ◇ · · ·

首都	しゅと	capital

---

52 市	city; market いち、シ	` 亠 亠 市 市 市

市 combines 亠, simplified from 止 stop (cf. 150), and 巾, depicting a balance. Thus 市 means market, where people stop and bargain until a balanced agreement is reached. An associated meaning is city.

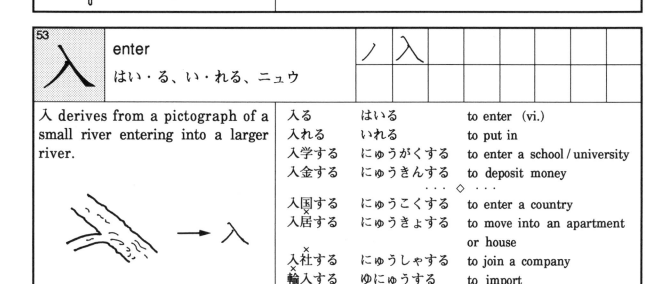

都市	とし	city
都市工学科	とし こうがっか	Department of Urban Engineering
京都市	きょうとし	the City of Kyoto

· · · ◇ · · ·

市場	いちば／しじょう	market, marketplace
市役所	しやくしょ	city / municipal office
市民	しみん	citizen
市長	しちょう	mayor

---

53 入	enter はい・る、い・れる、ニュウ	ノ 入

入 derives from a pictograph of a small river entering into a larger river.

入る	はいる	to enter (vi.)
入れる	いれる	to put in
入学する	にゅうがくする	to enter a school / university
入金する	にゅうきんする	to deposit money

· · · ◇ · · ·

入国する	にゅうこくする	to enter a country
入居する	にゅうきょする	to move into an apartment or house
入社する	にゅうしゃする	to join a company
輸入する	ゆにゅうする	to import
入会金	にゅうかいきん	entrance / enrollment fee

54 式

ceremony; style; formula

シキ

一　二　テ　王　式　式

式, which combines 弋 plough or weapon and 工 carpenter's ruler (cf. 43), means the style or form of something made with tools. Associated meanings are ceremony and formula.

式	しき	ceremony; formula
入学式	にゅうがくしき	entrance ceremony
· · · ◇ · · ·		
日本式	にほんしき	Japanese style / way
式（3）	しき さん	Equation (3)
卒業式	そつぎょうしき	graduation ceremony
結婚式	けっこんしき	wedding ceremony

55 文

literature; sentence; culture

ブン、モン

丶　一　ナ　文

文 was often used as a design on ancient clay pottery. Originally associated with design, it has now come to mean written passage, sentence, literature, and also culture.

文	ぶん	sentence, piece of writing
文学部	ぶんがくぶ	Faculty of Literature
· · · ◇ · · ·		
文化	ぶんか	culture
論文	ろんぶん	thesis, research paper
文部省	もんぶしょう	Ministry of Education, Science and Culture
文字	*もじ	letter or character

56 区

ward; district

ク

一　フ　又　区

区 derives from 區, which depicts many mouths or people (cf. 107 口) inside a boundary 匚. 区 thus indicates a district or ward.

文京区	ぶんきょうく	Bunkyo Ward
区間	くかん	interval (between two points along a railway or a road)
· · · ◇ · · ·		
区役所	くやくしょ	ward office
東京都区内	とうきょうとくない	within the twenty three wards of Tokyo

57 丁	counter for blocks of houses チョウ	一	丁							

丁 represents a sign showing a town or street name, and is used as a counter for blocks of houses, blocks of *tōfu*, and other food dishes.

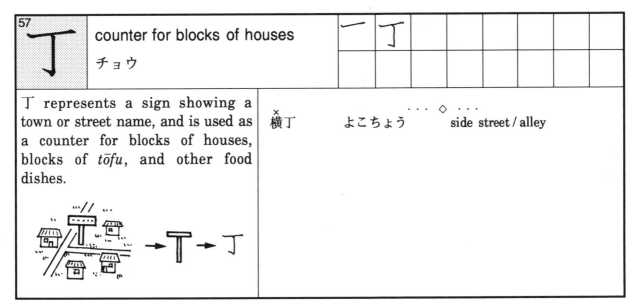

横丁	よこちょう	· · · ◇ · · · side street / alley

58 目	eye; suffix for ordinals め、モク	丨	冂	冂	目	目				

目 derives from a pictograph of an eye.

目	め	eye
一日目	いちにちめ	the first day
三丁目	さんちょうめ	the third block (in an address)
科目	かもく	course subject
		· · · ◇ · · ·
目上	めうえ	one's superior
目下	めした	one's subordinate
目次	もくじ	table of contents
目的	もくてき	purpose

4 PRACTICE

I. Write the readings of the following kanji in hiragana.

1. 東京大学　　2. 留学生　　3. 工学部　　4. 都市工学科

5. 三木先生　6. 専攻　　　7. 日本語　　8. 土木工学科

9. 入学式　　　10. 文京区　　11. 七丁目　　12. 東

13. 部分　　　　14. 先月　　　15. 入る　　　16. 科目

17. ピーターさんの　目は　大きいですね。

18. 科学や　文学を　べんきょうします。

19. 先週、京都へ　いきました。

20. わたしは　日本で　生まれました。

21. ここに　あなたの　生年月日を　かいてください。

22. フランス語で　みじかい　文を　かきました。

II. Fill in the blanks with appropriate kanji.

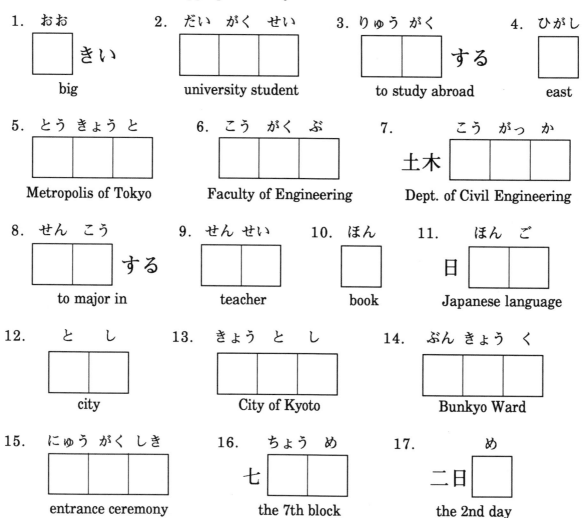

1. おお
□きい
big

2. だい がく せい
□□□
university student

3. りゅう がく
□□する
to study abroad

4. ひがし
□
east

5. とう きょう と
□□□
Metropolis of Tokyo

6. こう がく ぶ
□□□
Faculty of Engineering

7. こう がっ か
土木□□□
Dept. of Civil Engineering

8. せん こう
□□する
to major in

9. せん せい
□□
teacher

10. ほん
□
book

11. ほん ご
日□□
Japanese language

12. と し
□□
city

13. きょう と し
□□□
City of Kyoto

14. ぶん きょう く
□□□
Bunkyo Ward

15. にゅう がく しき
□□□
entrance ceremony

16. ちょう め
七□□
the 7th block

17. め
二日□
the 2nd day

定期券を 買います

IF YOU commute to work or school by train every day, you'll find it convenient to buy a commuter's pass. Good for one, three, or six months, the pass can be used as often as you like between the stations indicated on it. It normally costs about two-thirds the price of buying ordinary tickets, and only about one-third if you are a student. These passes can be purchased at major stations. In this lesson, you will learn how to fill in the application form to buy a commuter's pass. This knowledge will then help you fill in other kinds of forms as well.

1 INTRODUCTORY QUIZ

Look at the illustrations below and refer to the words in VOCABULARY. Then try the following quiz.

Ⅰ. The commuter's pass above shows all of the following information.
① It is valid between Yotsuya station and Shinjuku station.
② It is valid for 6 months, from March 14 to September 13, in the 4th year of Heisei (1992).
③ It costs ¥13,740.
④ It belongs to Mr. Sudoe.
⑤ Mr. Sudoe is a 20-year-old student.

Look over the commuter's pass below, and then answer the following questions.

1. この　定期券は ＿＿＿＿＿＿駅から ＿＿＿＿＿＿駅までです。

2. この　定期券は　平成5年＿＿月＿＿日から　平成5年＿＿月＿＿日までです。

3. この　定期券は ＿＿＿＿＿＿円です。

4. この　定期券は ＿＿＿＿＿＿さんのです。

5. この　人は　（ a. 学生です。　　b. 学生ではありません。）

Ⅱ. To buy a commuter's pass you need to fill in an application form like the one shown below. Try to fill in this application form as best you can.

定期券購入申込書

(お願い) ○氏名欄は、わくの中にはっきりと大きく書いて下さい。
○空欄に記入又は該当のものを○で囲んで下さい。
○お手もとの定期券は発行窓口へお渡し下さい。

氏　　　名	区　間	新三郷 駅　　根津 駅間
スドウ.ダニエル 様 30才 (男)女		（　　　　　　　　経由）
	使用開始日及び有効期間	平成 2 年 8 月 2 日から ①・3・6か月

| 住　　所 | 〒341 三郷市彦成 3-4-21-501 電話(0489)-59-1148 |

| 通勤先又は通学先 | 所在地 | 〒113 東京都 文京区 本郷 7-3-1 | このわく内には記入しないでください。 |
| | 名称 | 東京大学 電話(03)-3812-2111 | 種　類 | 通勤 (通学) |

定期券　申込書

氏　　　名	区　間	駅　　　　　駅間
様　　才 男女		
	使用開始日及び有効期間	平成　年　月　日から 1・3・6か月

| 住　　所 | 電話（　　　） |

| 通勤先又は通学先 | | |
| | 通勤　通学 | |

2 VOCABULARY

Study the readings and meanings of these words to help you understand the INTRODUC-TORY QUIZ.

1.	定期券	ていきけん	commuter's pass
2.	駅	えき	station
3.	～様	～さま	Mr. ~, Ms. ~, Miss ~, Mrs. ~
4.	通学	つうがく	commuting to school
5.	六本木	ろっぽんぎ	Roppongi (station)
6.	申込書	もうしこみしょ	application form
7.	氏名	しめい	full name
8.	男	おとこ	man
9.	女	おんな	woman
10.	～才	～さい	~ years old
11.	区間	くかん	interval (between two railway points)
12.	使用	しよう	use
13.	開始日	かいしび	starting date
14.	有効	ゆうこう	validity
15.	期間	きかん	period
16.	～か月	～かげつ	~ month(s)
17.	住所	じゅうしょ	address
18.	電話	でんわ	telephone
19.	通勤	つうきん	commuting to work
20.	通勤先	つうきんさき	one's place of work
21.	通学先	つうがくさき	one's school
22.	所在地	しょざいち	location
23.	名称	めいしょう	name
24.	種類	しゅるい	types

3 NEW CHARACTERS

Twenty-one characters are introduced in this lesson. Use the explanations to help you understand and remember the characters. Study the compound words to increase your vocabulary.

定 期 券 申 込 書 氏 名 男 女 才 駅 使 用 開
始 住 所 電 話 通

59 定	fix, decide; regular, definite テイ	﹀	﹀	宀	宁	宇	宇	字	定

定 combines the radical 宀 house, 一 one, and 止, a variation of 止 stop (cf. 150). Stopping in one part of a house implies a fixed place. Associated meanings include decide, regular and definite.

定休日	ていきゅうび	regular holiday, shop / company holiday
· · · ◇ · · ·		
定年	ていねん	retirement age
定価	ていか	list price
定員	ていいん	seating / passenger capacity; fixed number of personnel
未定	みてい	undecided, unscheduled

---

60 期	period of time, term キ	一	十	廿	甘	甘	其	其
		其	期	期	期			

期 combines 月 month and 其, a stiff basket made of tightly woven bamboo. From this association, 期 has come to mean fixed period of time or term.

定期	ていき	regular; abbreviation for 定期券 (commuter's pass)
学期	がっき	school term / semester
期間	きかん	term, period
· · · ◇ · · ·		
期限	きげん	deadline, time limit
短期大学	たんき だいがく	junior college
同期生	どうきせい	graduates in the same year

---

61 券	ticket ケン	﹅	﹀	丷	丷	半	关	券	券

券 combines 关 bamboo sheet marked with an ×, and 刀 sword or knife. Ancient Chinese would scratch a thin bamboo scroll with a knife and give one half to another person as a certificate. From this, 券 has come to mean ticket.

券	けん	ticket
定期券	ていきけん	commuter's pass
· · · ◇ · · ·		
乗車券	じょうしゃけん	train / bus ticket
指定券	していけん	seat reservation ticket
旅券	りょけん	passport

| 62 申 | say, report もう・す、シン | 丶 | 冂 | 日 | 日 | 申 | | |

申 derives from 电, which is part of the kanji for lightning 電 (cf. 77). One speaks to a superior with the same awe or fear one has in the presence of lightning. Thus 申 means say in a humble form.

申す	もうす	to say (humble form)
	・・・◇・・・	
申請する	しんせいする	to apply / petition for
申告する	しんこくする	to report, to notify

| 63 込 | be crowded; counted in こ・む | ノ | 入 | 込 | 込 | 込 | | |

込, which combines 入 enter (cf. 53) and 辶 proceed (cf. 16 週), is a kanji created in Japan. From its original meaning of enter or gather, 込 has come to mean counted or be crowded.

込む	こむ	to be crowded
申(し)込む	もうしこむ	to apply for (enrollment, etc.); to propose (marriage)
	・・・◇・・・	
払(い)込む	はらいこむ	to pay into
振(り)込む	ふりこむ	to transfer money by bank

| 64 書 | write; book か・く、ショ | コ | ヲ | ヨ | ヨ | 聿 | 書 | 書 |
| | | 書 | 書 | | | | | |

書 depicts a hand holding a brush and writing on a piece of paper.

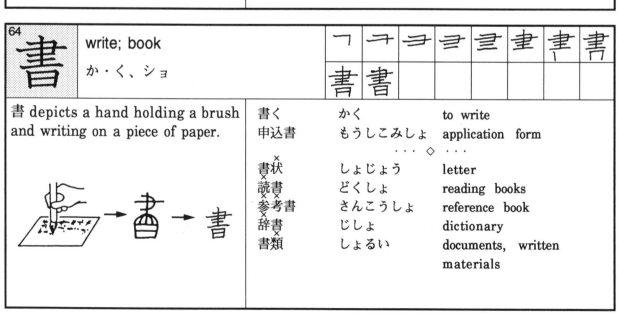

書く	かく	to write
申込書	もうしこみしょ	application form
	・・・◇・・・	
書状	しょじょう	letter
読書	どくしょ	reading books
参考書	さんこうしょ	reference book
辞書	じしょ	dictionary
書類	しょるい	documents, written materials

65 氏

family; surname

シ

ノ	ヒ	比	氏				

氏 derives from the shape of a sewing needle, suggesting a seam. Stitches in a seam follow one after another, like generations of a family. Thus 氏 means family and, by extension, family name.

スミス氏	スミスし	Mr./Ms./Miss/Mrs. Smith
	···◇···	

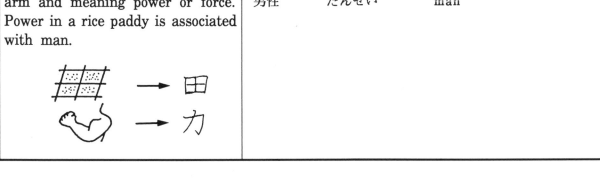

66 名

name; reputation

な、メイ

ノ	ク	タ	夕	名	名		

名 combines 夕, which depicts the moon above a mountain and means evening, and 口 mouth (cf.107), which implies speak. When it's difficult to recognize people on dark evenings, their names must be spoken aloud.

名前	なまえ	name
氏名	しめい	full name
名人	めいじん	expert, master
20名	20めい	twenty people
	···◇···	
名古屋	なごや	Nagoya
有名な	ゆうめいな	famous, well-known
名刺	めいし	business card, name card

67 男

man, male

おとこ、ダン

丨	冂	冂	用	田	男	男	

男 combines 田 rice paddy (cf. 87) and 力, depicting a strong man's arm and meaning power or force. Power in a rice paddy is associated with man.

男	おとこ	man, male
	···◇···	
男性	だんせい	man

68 女	woman おんな、ジョ	く	夂	女					

女 derives from a pictograph of a woman holding a baby in her arms.

女	おんな	woman, female
男女	だんじょ	men and women
・・・ ◇ ・・・		
女性	じょせい	woman

69 才	talent; age, ～ years old サイ	一	十	才					

才 derives from a pictograph of a floodgate made of timber, suggesting a useful resource. From this came the meaning of talent, which is something useful to have. 才 is also a simplified character for 歳, which is used to mean age for official documents and formal occasions.

25才／歳	25さい	twenty-five years old
・・・ ◇ ・・・		
天才	てんさい	genius

70 駅	station エキ	丨	厂	厂	匡	耳	馬	馬	馬
		馬	馬	馬¬	馬¬	馬尸	駅		

駅 combines 馬 horse and 尺, a unit of length deriving from the shape of stretched fingers. In the past, stations were placed at regular intervals for travelers and horses to stop and rest.

駅	えき	station
駅前	えきまえ	in front of a station
駅名	えきめい	station name
・・・ ◇ ・・・		
駅長	えきちょう	stationmaster
駅員	えきいん	station employee / staff
駅弁	えきべん	box lunch sold at a station
駅ビル	えきビル	station building

71 使 — use, messenger
つか・う、シ

使 combines 亻 man and 吏, a hand holding a brush and papers, representing a government officer. Thus 使 suggests a superior employing or using his officers, and has come to mean use in general.

使う	つかう	to use
大使	たいし	ambassador
・・・◇・・・		
使い方	つかいかた	how to use, directions for use
大使館	たいしかん	embassy

72 用 — use, usage; business
もち・いる、ヨウ

用 depicts a fence used to keep sheep in one place, and has come to mean use in general.

用	よう	something to do, business
使用する	しようする	to use
学生用	がくせいよう	for students
専用	せんよう	for private / exclusive use
・・・◇・・・		
用いる	もちいる	to use
用紙	ようし	blank form / paper
利用者	りようしゃ	user
採用する	さいようする	to adopt; to employ

73 開 — open
ひら・く、あ・く、あ・ける、カイ

開 depicts two hands 廾 (cf. 88 手) removing the bolt 一 from a gate 門 (cf. 181) in order to open it.

開く	ひらく	to open
開く	あく	to open (vi.)
開ける	あける	to open (vt.)
・・・◇・・・		
開店する	かいてんする	to open a shop; for a shop to open
開発する	かいはつする	to develop (vt.)

74 始 — begin, start
はじ・まる、はじ・める、シ

く	夕	女	女´	女ム	始	始	始

始 combines 女 woman (cf. 68) and 台 foundation. A woman is the foundation of all our beginnings.

始まる	はじまる	to start / begin (vi.)
始める	はじめる	to start / begin (vt.)
開始する	かいしする	to start / begin

. . . ◇ . . .

開始日	かいしび	starting date
始業式	しぎょうしき	opening ceremony for a new semester at school

75 住 — live
す・む、ジュウ

ノ	イ	イ´	仁	住	住	住

住, which combines 亻 man and 主 candle with a still flame, means stay still or live in one place. As part of other kanji, 主 often means stay still.

住む	すむ	to live

. . . ◇ . . .

住まい	すまい	residence, house
住民票	じゅうみんひょう	resident registration certificate
住宅	じゅうたく	house, residence

76 所 — place
ところ、ショ、（ジョ）

一	ラ	ヲ	戸	戸´	所	所	所

戸 derives from a pictograph of a door, and 斤 from that of an ax. The place to keep an ax is near the door.

所	ところ	place
住所	じゅうしょ	address
名所	めいしょ	famous place

. . . ◇ . . .

現住所	げんじゅうしょ	present address
所在地	しょざいち	location, address
近所	きんじょ	neighborhood

77 電	electricity デン	一	一	厂	币	雨	雨	雨	雨
		雷	雷	雷	雷	電			

電 is a variation of 雷 thunder, which combines 雨 rain and 田 rice paddy (cf. 87). 電 indicates lightning, and has come to mean electricity.

· · · ◇ · · ·

電気	でんき	electricity
電子	でんし	electron
電力	でんりょく	electric power
電池	でんち	battery
電報	でんぽう	telegram

---

78 話	speak, talk; story はな・す、はなし、ワ	、	二	言	言	言	言	言	言
		訂	訂	訂	話	話			

話, which combines 言 word or say and 舌 tongue, means speak or story.

話す	はなす	to talk, to speak
話	はなし	story, talk, speech
電話	でんわ	telephone

· · · ◇ · · ·

会話	かいわ	conversation
話題	わだい	topic, subject of conversation / speech
市外通話	しがい つうわ	out-of-town / long-distance call

---

79 通	go through, pass; commute とお・る、（どお・り）、ツウ	フ	マ	マ	予	予	予	甬	甬
		通	通						

通 combines ⻌ go (cf. 16 週) and 甬, a man putting a stick through a fence. Thus 通 means go through or pass.

通る	とおる	to pass, to go through
バス通り	バスどおり	street with bus service
通学する	つうがくする	to go to school
通学先	つうがくさき	one's school

· · · ◇ · · ·

通常	つうじょう	usually, normally
通勤する	つうきんする	to commute
交通	こうつう	traffic, transportation

4　PRACTICE

Ⅰ. Write the readings of the following kanji in hiragana.

1. 定 期 券　　2. 申 込 書　　3. 通 学　　4. 駅　　　　5. 氏 名

6. 男　　　　　7. 女　　　　　8. 〜 才　　9. 区 間　　10. 使 用

11. 開 始 日　12. 期 間　　　13. 住 所　　14. 電 話　　15. 定 休 日

16. 学 期　　　17. 通 る　　　18. 駅 名　　19. 大 使　　20. 所

21. 申 し 込 む　　　　　　　　22. あなたの　名前を　書いてください。

23. 駅前から　タクシーに　のりました。

24. いい　てんきです。　まどを　開けましょう。

25. クラスは　十時に　始まります。

26. わたしは　東京に　住んでいます。

27. きのうの　よる　ともだちと　電話で　話しました。

Ⅱ. Fill in the blanks with appropriate kanji.

1. か
□ く
to write

2. もうし こみ しょ
□□□
application form

3. てい き けん
□□□
commuter's pass

4. し
スミス □
Mr. Smith

5. だん じょ
□□
men and women

6. さい
30 □
30 years old

7. えき
□
station

8. つか
□ う
to use

9. し よう
□□ する
to use

10. す ところ
□ む □
place to live

11. めい しょ
□□
famous place

12. ひら
□ く
to open

13. はじ
□ める
to begin

14.
かい　し
□□ する
to begin

15.
どお
バス □ り
street with bus service

16.
つう
□ 学先
one's school

17.
はな
□ す
to talk

5 SUPPLEMENT

New Patient Form (used when visiting a doctor's office)

診 療 申 込 書

フリガナ												性別
患者氏名												男(M)・女(F)
生年月日	(M) (T) (S) (H) 明・大・昭・平 年 月 日					年齢		才				
現住所												
	郵便番号	□□□-□□		電話（　　）番号　　　－								
初診	年 月 日			職業：								
緊急時連絡先・電話番号												

▓▓ **REVIEW EXERCISE** ▓▓ Lessons 1–5

I. Connect the kanji and corresponding pictographs.

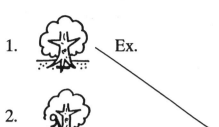

1. Ex.
2.
3.
4.
5.
6.
7.
8.

a. 日
b. 火
c. 水
d. 本
e. 休
f. 分
g. 金
h. 先
i. 式
j. 科
k. 門
l. 男
m. 書
n. 曜
o. 週
p. 祭

9.
10.
11.
12.
13.
14.
15.
16.

II. Choose the correct kanji for the given readings.

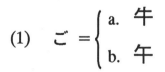

(1) ご = { a. 牛 b. 午 }

(2) と = { a. 都 b. 部 }

(3) かい = { a. 間 b. 開 }

(4) はん = { a. 半 b. 羊 }

(5) つき = { a. 月 b. 目 }

(6) こう = { a. 土 b. 工 }

(7) まん = { a. 方 b. 万 }

(8) つう = { a. 週 b. 通 }

(9) わ = { a. 話 b. 語 }

なに線に のりますか

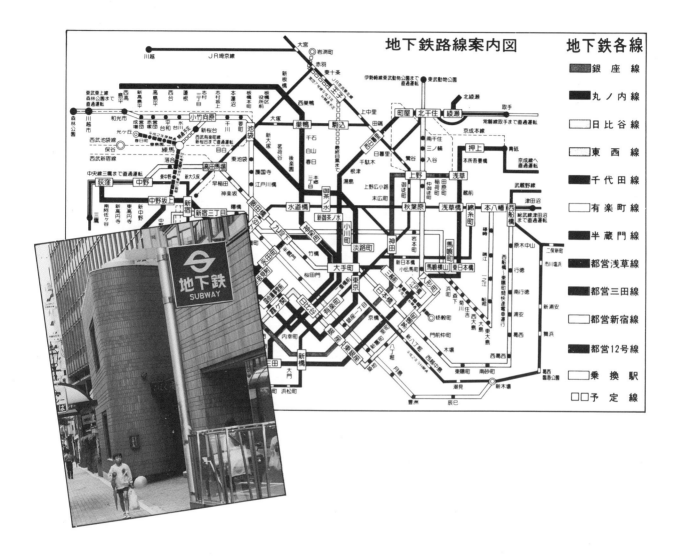

IN MAJOR cities in Japan, subways have become the primary means of transportation. The map above shows the subway lines and stations in Tokyo. The lines and their connections seem quite complicated, but most people still find the subway the most convenient way to get around. All lines are marked with a different color, and these colors are displayed on route maps and signs in the stations themselves. The Tokyo subway system consists of the Eidan Lines and the Toei Lines, and most of these also link up with the JR (Japan Railway) and private railway lines. Subway stations are easy to spot, because they are marked with big signs above station entrances, as shown in the photo above.

1 INTRODUCTORY QUIZ

Look at the illustration below and refer to the words in VOCABULARY. Then try the following quiz.

Ⅰ. Shown below is a simplified Tokyo subway map. If you live in Tokyo, you may recognize some of the kanji from signs. As you match the kanji and the readings for the following stations, enter the correct letters in the spaces provided.

1. ろっぽんぎ (　　)　　　2. おおてまち (　　)　　3. うえの (　　　)

4. とうきょう (　　)　　　5. しんじゅく (　　)　　6. ほんごうさんちょうめ (　　　)

a. 東京　　　　b. 新宿　　　　c. 大手町
d. 上野　　　　e. 本郷三丁目　　f. 六本木

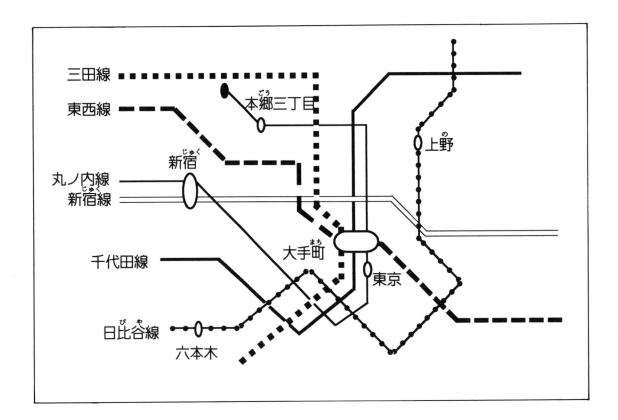

Ⅱ. Using the map above, identify the lines that pass through the following stations. Then enter the correct letters in the spaces provided.

1. 大手町 (　　) (　　) (　　) (　　)　　　2. 六本木　(　　)

3. 新宿 (　　) (　　)　　　　　　　　　　4. 東京　　(　　)

a. ひびや線　　b. しんじゅく線　　c. みた線
d. ちよだ線　　e. まるのうち線　　f. とうざい線

Ⅲ. As mentioned earlier, the subway lines in Tokyo are grouped into the Eidan Lines and the Toei Lines. Recognition of these kanji is important when selecting the appropriate ticket vending machine. Suppose you are taking the following lines, marked 1, 2, and 3. Referring to the information below, choose the appropriate machine, (a) or (b).

1. 三田線は （ a. 都営　　b. 営団 ）線です。
2. 東西線は （ a. 都営　　b. 営団 ）線です。
3. 丸ノ内線は （ a. 都営　　b. 営団 ）線です。

　えいだんせん：　丸ノ内線、千代田線、東西線
　　とえいせん：　三田線、新宿線

2 VOCABULARY

Study the readings and meanings of these words to help you understand the INTRODUC-TORY QUIZ.

1. なに線	なに せん	what line
2. 地下鉄	ち か てつ	subway
3. 六本木	ろっ ぽん ぎ	Roppongi (station)
4. 大手町	おお て まち	Otemachi (station)
5. 上野	うえ の	Ueno (station)
6. 新宿	しん じゅく	Shinjuku (station)
7. 本郷三丁目	ほん ごう さん ちょう め	Hongo-Sanchome (station)
8. 日比谷線	ひ び や せん	Hibiya Line
9. 新宿線	しん じゅく せん	Shinjuku Line
10. 三田線	み た せん	Mita Line
11. 千代田線	ち よ だ せん	Chiyoda Line
12. 丸ノ内線	まる の うち せん	Marunouchi Line
13. 東西線	とう ざい せん	Tozai Line
14. 営団線	えい だん せん	Eidan Line (semi-governmental)
15. 都営線	と えい せん	Toei Line (municipal)

3 NEW CHARACTERS

Fourteen characters are introduced in this lesson. Use the explanations to help you understand and remember the characters. Study the compound words to increase your vocabulary.

地 下 鉄 丸 内 線 代 田 手 西 営 団 新 上

---

80 地	land, earth	一 十 土 𡈼 圤 地
	チ、ジ	

地 combines 土 modified from 土 ground (cf. 31) and 也 snake. Since snakes slither on the ground, 地 has come to mean land or earth.

土地	とち	(piece of) land
地名	ちめい	place name
	···◇···	
地図	ちず	map
地球	ちきゅう	the earth, the globe
地震	じしん	earthquake

---

81 下	below, under, down, lower; fall, descent	一 丁 下
	した、くだ・る、カ、ゲ	

To indicate below, under, or down, the ancient Chinese drew a dot below a line. This was later modified to 下.

下	した	below, under, down, lower
下り	くだり	down, descent; abbreviation for 下り電車 (out-bound train)
地下	ちか	underground
	···◇···	
下着	したぎ	underwear
下町	したまち	the traditional shopping, entertainment and residential districts (of Tokyo); downtown
下水	げすい	sewerage
千円以下	せんえん いか	one thousand yen or less

82 鉄 — iron / テツ

ノ 入 亼 亽 牟 牟 金 金 金¹ 金¹ 金⁻ 鉄⁻ 鉄

鉄, which combines 金 metal (cf. 30) and 失 lose, means iron, a metal that loses its value when it rusts.

鉄	てつ	iron, steel
地下鉄	ちかてつ	subway
· · · ◇ · · ·		
鉄道	てつどう	railway
私鉄	してつ	private railway line / company

83 丸 — circle, round / まる、まる・い

ノ 九 丸

丸, which depicts a man rounding his back to enter a cave, means round. An associated meaning is circle.

丸	まる	circle
丸い	まるい	round, circular, spherical
· · · ◇ · · ·		

84 内 — inside / うち、ナイ

｜ 冂 内 内

内 depicts a man 人 inside a house 冂, meaning inside.

都内	とない	inside Tokyo
年内	ねんない	within the year
内科	ないか	internal medicine unit; internal medicine
· · · ◇ · · ·		
内側	うちがわ	inside
学内便	がくないびん	campus mail
家内	かない	my wife
市内	しない	inside a city, civic

85 線 — line / セン

く	幺	幺	彳	糸	糸	糸'	糸
糸'	糸'	絈	紵	綧	線	線	

線 combines 糸, twisted bundle of thread, 白 white (cf. 11 百), and 水 water. 泉 means spring, whose water is clean and white. Water from a spring flows in a line like thread.

線	せん	line
丸ノ内線	まるのうちせん	Marunouchi Line
JR線	JRせん	Japan Railway Line
内線	ないせん	extension (telephone)
	· · · ◇ · · ·	
国内線	こくないせん	domestic route / flight
国際線	こくさいせん	international route / flight
新幹線	しんかんせん	Shinkansen (bullet train)
無線 タクシー	むせん タクシー	radio taxi

86 代 — substitute, replace; price; generation / か・わる、よ、ダイ

ノ	イ	仁	代	代		

代, which combines 亻 man and 弋 weapon (cf. 54 式), came to mean substitute from the idea of an army getting stronger as weapons were substituted for man power. When buying things, money is substituted for a commodity; thus 代 also means price. An associated meaning is generation.

代(わ)りに	かわりに	instead
代々木	よよぎ	Yoyogi (place)
バス代	バスだい	bus fare
時代	じだい	period, epoch, era
代金	だいきん	price, charge
	· · · ◇ · · ·	
電気代	でんきだい	electricity charges
現代	げんだい	present age, modern times
世代	せだい	generation
代理人	だいりにん	deputy, agent, substitute

87 田 — rice field, paddy / た、（だ）

丨	冂	冊	田	田		

田 derives from a pictograph of a rice field.

田	た	rice field, paddy
三田線	みたせん	Mita Line
千代田線	ちよだせん	Chiyoda Line
	· · · ◇ · · ·	
田中さん	たなかさん	Mr./Ms./Miss/Mrs. Tanaka
本田さん	ほんださん	Mr./Ms./Miss/Mrs. Honda
小田急線	おだきゅうせん	Odakyu Line

88 手	hand て、シュ	ノ ニ 二 手						

手 derives from a pictograph of a hand. All the elements shown below are used to refer to hand.

寸 又 乂 ⇒ ヨ 又 扌 ナ

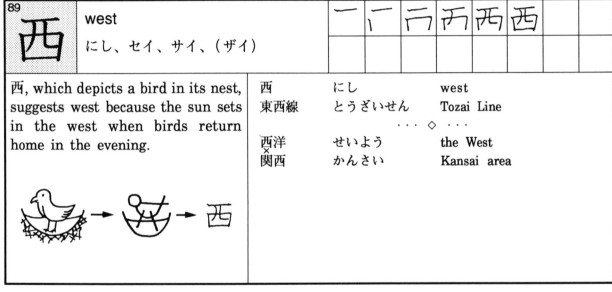

手	て	hand
山手線	やまのてせん	Yamanote Line
大手町	おおてまち	Otemachi (place)
	· · · ◇ · · ·	
手紙	てがみ	letter
手数料	てすうりょう	fee, charge, commission
歌手	かしゅ	singer
助手	じょしゅ	research associate, assistant
選手	せんしゅ	athlete

89 西	west にし、セイ、サイ、（ザイ）	一 一 厂 西 西 西						

西, which depicts a bird in its nest, suggests west because the sun sets in the west when birds return home in the evening.

西	にし	west
東西線	とうざいせん	Tozai Line
	· · · ◇ · · ·	
西洋	せいよう	the West
関西	かんさい	Kansai area

90 営	perform, manage エイ	丶 丷 ツ 𠆢 𫝀 𫝀 営 営
		営 営 営 営

営 derives from 營. 𫝀 indicates house 宀 with lights 火 on, and 呂 represents rooms. From this, 営 has come to mean perform work or manage business in an office.

都営地下鉄	とえい ちかてつ	metropolitan subway
市営	しえい	municipally-managed
	· · · ◇ · · ·	
経営者	けいえいしゃ	manager, executive

91 団 — group
ダン

1	冂	円	団	団	団		

団 derives from 團, which combines 囗 enclosure and 專 special or exclusive (cf. 46). Thus 團 or 団 means group of people sharing a special purpose or interest.

営団線	えいだんせん	Eidan line (semi-governmental subway)
バレエ団	バレエだん	ballet company
	… ◇ …	
団体	だんたい	group of persons / organizations
集団	しゅうだん	group
公団	こうだん	public corporation
団子	だんご	dumpling

92 新 — new
あたら・しい 、シン

'	十	六	立	立	立	辛	辛
辛	亲	新	新	新			

新 combines 立 stand (cf. 167), 木 tree, and 斤 ax (cf. 76 所). From the idea of cutting a standing tree with an ax to produce fresh timber, 新 has come to mean new. Another version says that standing trees are cut to clear new land.

新しい	あたらしい	new
新年	しんねん	the New Year
新入生	しんにゅうせい	new student / pupil
新宿	しんじゅく	Shinjuku (place)
	… ◇ …	
新人	しんじん	newcomer, new face
新住所	しんじゅうしょ	new address
新学期	しんがっき	new term / semester
新聞	しんぶん	newspaper

93 上 — above, on, up, upper; rise
うえ、のぼ・る、ジョウ

1	卜	上					

To indicate above, on, or up, the ancient Chinese drew a dot above a line. This was later modified to 上.

● → 丄 → 上

上	うえ	on, above, up, upper
年上	としうえ	elder
上野	うえの	Ueno (place)
上り	のぼり	up, ascent
上下	じょうげ	top and bottom, upper and lower, up and down
	… ◇ …	
上り電車	のぼり でんしゃ	in-bound train
屋上	おくじょう	housetop, roof
五人以上	ごにん いじょう	five people or more
上級	じょうきゅう	advanced course

80

4 PRACTICE

I. Write the readings of the following kanji in hiragana.

1. 地下鉄　　　2. 六本木　　　3. 大手町(まち)　　4. 上野(の)

5. 新宿(じゅく)　6. 日比(ひ)谷(や)線　7. 三田線　　8. 千代田線

9. 丸ノ内線　10. 東西線　　11. 営団線　　12. 都営線

13. 地名　　　14. 下り　　　15. 内線　　　16. 時代

17. 西　　　　18. 新年　　　19. 上り

20. 東の　そらに、丸い　月が　でています。

21. 上田さんは　わたしより　二つ　年上です。

22. 新宿(じゅく)には　新しい　ビルが　たくさん　あります。

II. Fill in the blanks with appropriate kanji.

1. した
below

2. ち　か
underground

3. てつ
iron

4. ち　か　てつ
subway

5. だい
バス
bus fare

6. ない
都
inside Tokyo

7. た　せん
三
Mita Line

8. て
大きい
big hand

9. にし

west

10. ざい　せん
東
Tozai Line

11. だん
バレエ
ballet company

12. しん
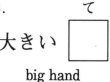 入生
new student

13. えい
市
municipally-managed

14. うえ

above

15. じょう　げ
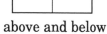
above and below

きっぷを かいましょう

きっぷうりばご案内

JR 1,590 円区間までは
自動きっぷうりば でお求めください。

JR 1,850 円区間以上は 窓口で
お求めください。

きっぷうりばご案内

特急券・寝台券・指定席券
ワイド・ミニ周遊券・ギフトカード

1,590円をこえる区間のJR全線
定期券・回数券・自由席特急券
急行券・普通列車グリーン券

上記のきっぷは窓口でお求めください。

EXCEPT FOR long-distance tickets, ordinary subway and railroad tickets are valid only on the day of issue. Coupon tickets are also available for about a 10% discount. Since different kinds of tickets are required by the Eidan, Toei, JR, and private lines, care should be taken to use the proper vending machines in stations serving many lines. Long-distance tickets that cost more than 2,000 yen are usually purchased at ticket windows. At many stations, automated ticket gates are replacing conventional ones, as seen in the photo above.

1 INTRODUCTORY QUIZ

Look at the illustration below and refer to the words in VOCABULARY. Then try the following quiz.

Ⅰ. Below right is a simplified route map of the Yamanote (▬) and Chuo (▨) Lines. The stations marked ◎ are connecting stations. The Yamanote Line is a loop, and it takes about an hour to make a complete circle. The Chuo Line starts from Tokyo station, cuts through the center of the Yamanote Line, and goes as far as Takao, about 50 kilometers from its starting point. Study the fare chart at Shinjuku station, and then answer the questions.

自動きっぷうりば　ご案内

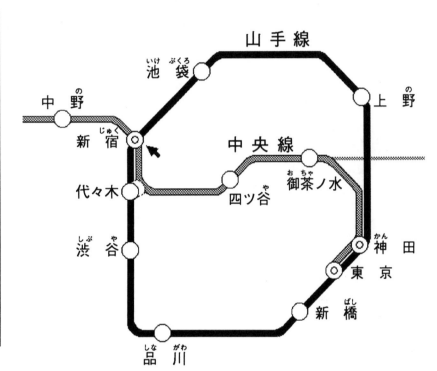

駅　　名	料金（円）
代々木	120
渋谷	150
池袋	150
品川	190
上野	190
新橋	190
東京	190
中野	150
四ツ谷	150
御茶ノ水	160
神田	160

1. 新宿から　つぎの　駅までは　いくらですか。

    a. しんばし　　（　　　　　）円　　　　b. よよぎ　　（　　　　　）円

    c. おちゃのみず（　　　　　）円　　　　d. なかの　　（　　　　　）円

2. 山手線と　中央線の　連絡駅は　どれと　どれですか。

    a. 新宿　　b. 上野　　c. 御茶ノ水　　d. 東京

Ⅱ. Shown below are various kinds of ordinary and coupon tickets for the JR lines, purchased at Shinjuku station. There are two types of coupon tickets: one for a specified interval along the lines, and the other for unlimited distance on the Yamanote Line. The child's ticket looks the same as the adult's ticket, but it is marked with kanji meaning "small". Match the appropriate ticket to each statement below, and write the correct letters (a～e) in the spaces provided.

a

d

b

e

c
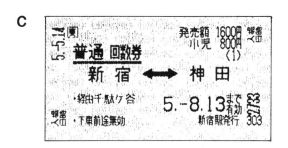

Ex. （ a ）は　新宿から　東京行きの　きっぷです。

1. 新宿から　代々木行きは　大人は　120円、　こどもは　60円です。

　　大人の　きっぷは　（　）で、こどもの　きっぷは　（　）です。

2. （　）は　この　区間だけの　回数券です。

3. （　）は　山手線内の　全線の　回数券です。

2 VOCABULARY

Study the readings and meanings of these words to help you understand the INTRODUC-TORY QUIZ.

1.	きっぷ		ticket
2.	代々木	よ よ ぎ	Yoyogi (station) (*See L2, 23 時)
3.	自動	じ どう	automatic
4.	うりば		(ticket) vending area
5.	(ご)案内	(ご) あん ない	information
6.	駅名	えき めい	station name
7.	料金	りょう きん	fare
8.	渋谷	しぶ や	Shibuya (station)
9.	池袋	いけ ぶくろ	Ikebukuro (station)
10.	品川	しな がわ	Shinagawa (station)
11.	新橋	しん ばし	Shinbashi (station)
12.	四ツ谷	よ つ や	Yotsuya (station)
13.	御茶ノ水	お ちゃ の みず	Ochanomizu (station)
14.	神田	かん だ	Kanda (station)
15.	山手線	やま の て せん	Yamanote Line
16.	中央線	ちゅう おう せん	Chuo Line
17.	連絡	れん らく	connection
18.	～行き	～ い き／ゆ き	bound for ~
19.	大人	おとな	adult
20.	小	しょう	abbreviation for child
21.	こども		child
22.	回数券	かい すう けん	coupon ticket
23.	山手線内	やま の て せん ない	within the Yamanote Line
24.	全線	ぜん せん	all along the line
25.	均一	きん いつ	uniformity, equality

3 NEW CHARACTERS

Twelve characters are introduced in this lesson. Use the explanations to help you understand and remember the characters. Study the compound words to increase your vocabulary.

山 中 央 連 絡 自 動 小 人 全 行 回

94 山 mountain
やま、サン、（ザン）

┃	山	山					

山 derives from a pictograph of mountains.

山	やま	mountain
山手線	やまのてせん	Yamanote Line
火山	かざん	volcano
··· ◇ ···		
山田さん	やまだ×さん	Mr. / Ms. / Miss / Mrs. Yamada
富士山	ふじさん	Mt. Fuji

95 中 middle, inside; throughout
なか、チュウ、（ジュウ）

┃	冖	口	中				

中 depicts a board with a rod through its center.

中	なか	the inside, the interior
中野×	なかの	Nakano (place)
使用中	しようちゅう	in use, Occupied
一日中	いちにちじゅう	all day long
日本中	にほんじゅう	throughout Japan
··· ◇ ···		
中学×	ちゅうがく	junior high school
中心×	ちゅうしん	center
中級×	ちゅうきゅう	intermediate course
中古	ちゅうこ	used, secondhand

96 央 center, middle
オウ

┃	冖	口	央	央			

央 depicts a man standing with arms outstretched in the middle of a house.

中央	ちゅうおう	the center, the middle
中央区	ちゅうおうく	Chuo Ward
中央線	ちゅうおうせん	Chuo Line
··· ◇ ···		

97 連

connect, link; take along

つ・れる、レン

一 ／ 「 﨑 百 亘 車 ` 車 連 連

連 means connect or link, because vehicles 車 (cf. 106) on a road 辶 (cf. 16 週) follow one after another like links in a chain.

連れて行く	つれて いく	to take (someone) along / with
連休	れんきゅう	consecutive holidays
· · · ◇ · · ·		
関連	かんれん	relation, connection
国連	こくれん	abbreviation for 国際連合 (the United Nations)

98 絡

get tangled; connect

から・む、ラク

く 乡 幺 幺 糸 糸 糸 絲 絞 絡 絡 絡

絡 combines 糸 thread (cf. 85 線) and 各, which by itself means each (cf. 121) but here indicates a knotted thread. A thread with knots gets tangled easily. An associated meaning is connect.

連絡する	れんらくする	to connect with, to make contact
連絡先	れんらくさき	where to contact
連絡駅	れんらくえき	connecting station, junction
· · · ◇ · · ·		
絡む	からむ	to get tangled
連絡口	れんらくぐち	connection gate
連絡通路	れんらく つうろ	connecting passageway

99 自

self

ジ、シ

丿 亻 白 白 白 自

自 derives from a pictograph of a nose. In Japan, pointing at one's nose indicates I or me.

自分	じぶん	oneself, one's own
· · · ◇ · · ·		
自由な	じゆうな	free, unrestricted
自宅	じたく	one's own home / house
自然	しぜん	nature

---

100 動 move
うご・く 、ドウ

ノ　ニ　一　台　台　台　重　重　重　動　動

動 combines 重, man standing on a pile of heavy things on the ground, and 力 force (cf. 67 男). Even heavy things will move if great forces are exerted on them.

重 → 重 → 重

動く	うごく	to move (vi.)
自動	じどう	automatic
‥‥◇‥‥		
手動	しゅどう	manually operated, hand-powered
×運動する	うんどうする	to exercise, to campaign, to move

---

101 小 small, little
こ、ちい・さい、ショウ

丿　小　小

小 depicts a stick shaved on both sides to make it slender and small.

⊠ → 小 → 小

小さい	ちいさい	small, little
小学生	しょうがくせい	school children
‥‥◇‥‥		
小×包	こづつみ	parcel
小×説	しょうせつ	novel
小児科	しょうにか	pediatrics
大小	だいしょう	large and small, size

---

102 人 human being; person
ひと、ジン、ニン

丿　人

人 derives from a pictograph of a man. When used as a radical, 人 is written 亻.

亻 → 人 → 人

人	ひと	person
日本人	にほんじん	a Japanese
本人	ほんにん	the person himself / herself, the said person
大人	*おとな	adult
二人	*ふたり	two people
‥‥◇‥‥		
×主人	しゅじん	husband; shop owner
人間	にんげん	human being

---

103 全 all, whole; entirely
ゼン

ノ 入 △ 仝 全 全

全 represents a mound ㅅ of earth 土 containing everything or covering the whole area underneath.

全線	ぜんせん	all (train / bus) lines, all along the line
全学	ぜんがく	the whole university
全部	ぜんぶ	all, whole

· · · ◇ · · ·

全国	ぜんこく	the whole country
全体	ぜんたい	the whole
全員	ぜんいん	all members
完全な	かんぜんな	perfect, complete

---

104 行 go; line (of a text)
い・く／ゆ・く、コウ、ギョウ

ノ ク ネ 彳 彳 行 行

行 derives from the shape of a crossroad, meaning go. The radical 彳 refers to go or a road.

十 → 彳 → 行

行く	いく／ゆく	to go
行き先	いきさき／ゆきさき	destination of a journey, one's whereabouts
三行目	さんぎょうめ	the third line (on a page)

· · · ◇ · · ·

| ～行(き) | ～いき／ゆき | bound for ~ |
| 旅行する | りょこうする | to travel, to make a trip |

---

105 回 go around; times
まわ・る、まわ・す、カイ

丨 冂 冂 冋 回 回

回 derives from a pictograph of a whirlpool, which goes around in circles.

◎ → 回 → 回

回る	まわる	to turn / go round, to make a tour
回す	まわす	to turn / move / pass (something) round
回数券	かいすうけん	coupon ticket
四回目	よんかいめ	the fourth time

· · · ◇ · · ·

前回	ぜんかい	the last time
次回	じかい	the next time
回送	かいそう	out-of-service car / train

4 PRACTICE

Ⅰ. Write the readings of the following kanji in hiragana.

1. 代々木   2. 自動   3. 中野   4. 山手線   5. 中央線

6. 連絡   7. ～行き   8. 大人   9. 小   10. 回数券

11. 全線   12. 使用中 13. 日中   14. 中央   15. 自分

16. 小学生 17. 日本人 18. 一人   19. 二人   20. 三人

21. 回す   22. バスの　中で　ともだちに　あいました。

23. 五月の　連休は　どこへ　行きますか。　山へ　行きます。

24. 日曜日は　エレベーターが　動きません。

25. 小さい　駅には　とまりません。   26. 三行目を　よんでください。

Ⅱ. Fill in the blanks with appropriate kanji.

1. やま

□ 本さん
Mr./Ms. Yamamoto

2. ざん

火 □
volcano

3. なか

へやの □
inside a room

4. じゅう

日本 □
throughout Japan

5. ちゅう おう

□□ 区
Chuo Ward

6. つ　　い

□ れて □ く
to take (someone) with

7. れん らく

□□ 駅
connecting station

8. うご

□ く
to move

9. じ どう

□□ ドア
automatic door

10. ちい　　ひと

□ さい □
small person

11. 　　じん

メキシコ □
a Mexican

12. にん

本 □
the said person

13. い

□ き先
destination

14. ぎょう

九 □ 目
the 9th line

15. ぜん

□ 部
all

16. まわ

□ る
to turn round

17. かい

四 □ 目
the 4th time

電車に のりましょう

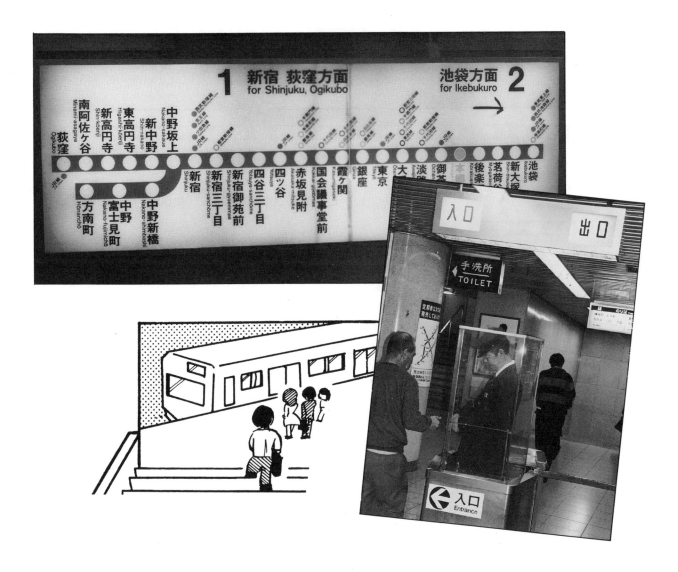

AFTER BUYING a ticket, finding the right platform can be a problem. Near the ticket gates in the station, there are guide boards that show all the stations along the line, and indicate the station where you are and the platform numbers for different destinations, as illustrated above. If you take the Marunouchi Line from Tokyo station, for example, the platforms will be marked 1 新宿方面 and 2 池袋方面. Guide boards on the platforms show the terminal stations and other major stations along the way. Thus, to go from Tokyo to Yotsuya, you will need to recognize at least three signs: 東京, 四ツ谷, and 新宿, and proceed to platform number 1.

1 INTRODUCTORY QUIZ

Look at the illustration below and refer to the words in VOCABULARY. Then try the following quiz.

Suppose this is Tokyo station. Look at the signs and choose the correct answers.

1. 駅の　ホームには　（ a. 入口　　b. 出口 ）から　はいります。
2. 新宿^{じゅく}　行きは　（ a. 1　　b. 2.）ばんせんです。
3. 大手町^{まち}　方面は　（ a. 1　　b. 2 ）番線です。
4. 四ツ谷^や　方面の　電車は　（ a. 1　　b. 2 ）番線です。

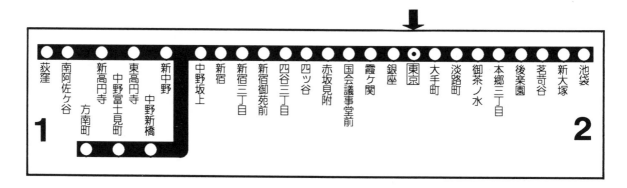

92

2 ☐ VOCABULARY

Study the readings and meanings of these words to help you understand the INTRODUC-TORY QUIZ.

1. 電車   でん しゃ   train
2. ホーム   platform
3. 入口   いり ぐち   entrance
4. 出口   で ぐち   exit
5. ～番線   ～ ばん せん   track no. ~
6. ～方面   ～ ほう めん   bound for ~
7. 四ッ谷   よ つ や   Yotsuya (station)

3 ☐ NEW CHARACTERS

Six characters are introduced in this lesson. Use the explanations to help you understand and remember the characters. Study the compound words to increase your vocabulary.

車 口 出 方 面 番

106 車	wheel, car, vehicle くるま、シャ	一 ｢ 一 一 一 一 車

車 derives from a pictograph of a carriage with wheels, meaning wheel or car.

車	くるま	car, wheel
電車	でんしゃ	train
車内	しゃない	the inside of a car / train

··· ◇ ···

自動車	じどうしゃ	automobile
自転車	じてんしゃ	bicycle
下車する	げしゃする	to get off (a train/car)

107 口 — mouth — くち、（ぐち）、コウ

Stroke order: 丨 冂 口

口 derives from a pictograph of a mouth. Associated meanings include opening, entrance, exit, and man.

口	くち	mouth; opening
入口	いりぐち	entrance
東口	ひがしぐち	east exit
中央口	ちゅうおうぐち	central exit
人口	じんこう	population
⋯ ◇ ⋯		
改札口	かいさつぐち	ticket gate, wicket
口座	こうざ	bank account
窓口	まどぐち	window (in a public office, bank, or station)

108 出 — go out, come out; take out; send; leave — で・る、だ・す、シュツ、（シュッ）

Stroke order: 丨 屮 屮 出 出

出 depicts a plant coming out of the ground a little more than the plant in the kanji 土 (cf. 31).

出る	でる	to go/come out
出口	でぐち	exit
出入口	でいりぐち	doorway, entrance and exit
出す	だす	to take something out; to send (a letter); to submit
⋯ ◇ ⋯		
出前	でまえ	ordering out for food
提出する	ていしゅつする	to submit
輸出する	ゆしゅつする	to export
出席する	しゅっせきする	to attend, to be present
出国する	しゅっこくする	to leave the country

109 方 — direction, side; method; person — かた、（がた）、ホウ、（ポウ）

Stroke order: 丶 亠 方 方

方 derives from a pictograph of a plow with a handle stretching out on both sides as if indicating two directions. An associated meaning is method.

書き方	かきかた	how to write, (way of) writing
この方	このかた	this gentleman / lady
地方	ちほう	region, locality, district, the provinces
一方通行	いっぽう つうこう	one-way traffic
⋯ ◇ ⋯		
夕方	ゆうがた	evening
方向	ほうこう	direction
方言	ほうげん	dialect

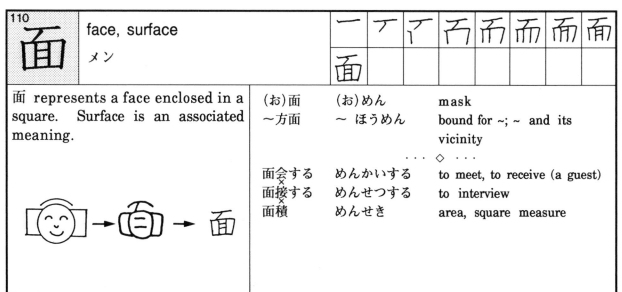

110

面 face, surface

メン

一	丆	广	丏	而	而	而	面
面							

面 represents a face enclosed in a square. Surface is an associated meaning.

(お)面	(お)めん	mask
～方面	～ ほうめん	bound for ~; ~ and its vicinity
	･･･ ◇ ･･･	
面会する	めんかいする	to meet, to receive (a guest)
面接する	めんせつする	to interview
面積	めんせき	area, square measure

111

番 number, turn; keep watch

バン

ノ	八	勹	厺	平	乎	釆	釆
番	番	番	番				

番 combines 釆 hand sowing seeds, and 田 rice paddy. Farmers keep watch over the paddy in turn until harvest time. Thus 番 means keeping watch, turn, and also number when the order of something is indicated.

一番	いちばん	no. 1, the most
二番目	にばんめ	the second
三番線	さんばんせん	track / platform no. 3
番地	ばんち	number of a house, address
	･･･ ◇ ･･･	
交番	こうばん	police box
順番	じゅんばん	order, one's turn
番組	ばんぐみ	TV / radio program
当番	とうばん	person on duty / watch

4 PRACTICE

Ⅰ. Write the readings of the following kanji in hiragana.

1. 電車　2. 入口　3. 出口　　4. ～番線　5. ～方面

6. 車　　　7. 車内　8. 中央口　9. 人口　　10. 出入口

11. 書き方　　12. 地方　　13. 一方通行　14. 番地

15. 口を　大きく　開けて　話してください。

16. 山と　山の　間から　日が　出てきました。

17. この方は　どなたですか。

18. お祭りで　お面を　かいました。

Ⅱ. Fill in the blanks with appropriate kanji.

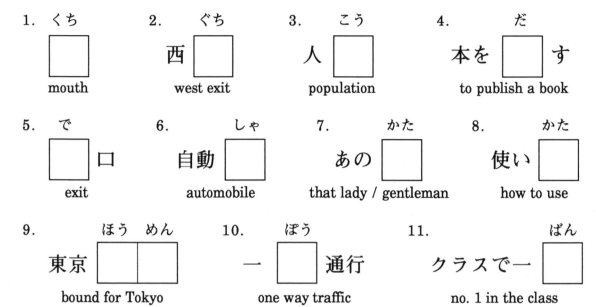

1. くち

　□

mouth

2. ぐち

西□

west exit

3. こう

人□

population

4. だ

本を□す

to publish a book

5. で

□口

exit

6. しゃ

自動□

automobile

7. かた

あの□

that lady / gentleman

8. かた

使い□

how to use

9. ほう　めん

東京□□

bound for Tokyo

10. ぽう

一□通行

one way traffic

11. ばん

クラスで一□

no. 1 in the class

12. ばん

二□線

platform no.2

駅の中

HAVE YOU ever been frustrated because you cannot understand the signs in stations? When you need to wash your hands, you'll look for the sign お手洗い. And once you reach it, you have to face another dilemma: which doorway to enter... If you take a taxi or bus from the station, which exit do you use? 東口 or 西口? And when you want to buy coupon tickets, you must find the appropriate ticket machine. Fortunately, most of these problems are solved when you understand the signs.

1 INTRODUCTORY QUIZ

Look at the illustration below and refer to the words in VOCABULARY. Then try the following quiz.

Ⅰ. The station below has ticket vending machines, an information desk, washrooms, information about taxis, and an emergency notice. Fill in the spaces provided with the correct letters (a～f).

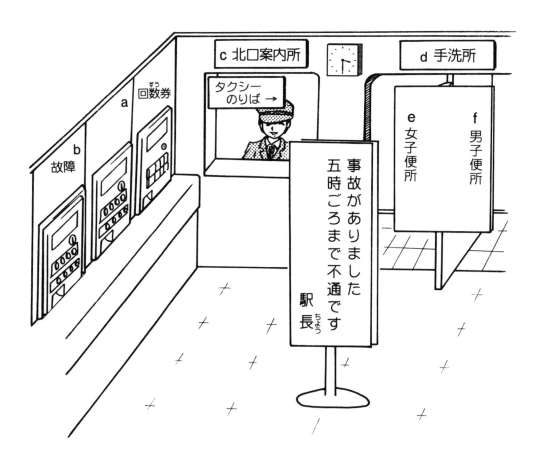

1. 駅の　あんないじょは　（　　）です。

2. おとこの　人の　トイレは　（　　）です。

3. おんなの　人の　お手洗いは　（　　）に　あります。

4. きっぷは　（　　）で　かいます。

Ⅱ. Choose the correct answers.

1. 電車は　すぐに　きますか。　（ a. はい。　b. いいえ。）

2. どうしてですか。　（ a. じこが　あった　　b. 日曜日だ ）からです。

3. 電車は　なん時ごろに　きますか。　（ a. 3時　　b. 5時 ）ごろに　きます。

4. きっぷうりばの　（ a.　　b. ）の　*きかいは　使えません。　　　　（*machine）

5. ここは　（ a. きた口　　b. みなみ口 ）です。

2 VOCABULARY

Study the readings and the meanings of these words to help you understand the INTRODUCTORY QUIZ.

1. 案内所　　　　　あん ない じょ　　　　　information desk
2. 男子　　　　　　だん し　　　　　　　　gentlemen
3. 便所　　　　　　べん じょ　　　　　　　lavatory
4. 女子　　　　　　じょ し　　　　　　　　ladies
5. (お)手洗い　　　(お) て あらい　　　　washroom, toilet
6. 手洗所　　　　　て あらい じょ　　　　washroom, toilet (formal)
7. 事故　　　　　　じ こ　　　　　　　　accident
8. 不通　　　　　　ふ つう　　　　　　　interruption of train service
9. 故障　　　　　　こ しょう　　　　　　out of order
10. 北口　　　　　　きた ぐち　　　　　　north exit
11. 南口　　　　　　みなみ ぐち　　　　　south exit

3 NEW CHARACTERS

Nine characters are introduced in this lesson. Use the explanations to help you understand and remember the characters. Study the compound words to increase your vocabulary.

北　南　案　便　洗　子　事　故　不

112 北	north きた、ホク、(ボク)、(ホッ)	一 　十 　土 　北 　北			

北 derives from a pictograph of two men sitting back to back and facing opposite directions. Men usually prefer facing the sun or south. Thus 北 has come to mean north, which is the opposite of south.

北	きた	north
北口	きたぐち	north exit
東北地方	とうほく ちほう	Tohoku district
北部	ほくぶ	northern district / part
· · · ◇ · · ·		
南北	なんぼく	south and north
北国	きたぐに	northern provinces / country
北米	ほくべい	North America
北海道	ほっかいどう	Hokkaido (island, district)

113 南 south

みなみ、ナン

一 十 ナ 广 占 内 内 南
南

南 depicts a plant inside a shed. Since plants turn to face the south, 南 has come to mean south.

南	みなみ	south
南口	みなみぐち	south exit
東南アジア	とうなん アジア	Southeast Asia
東西南北	とうざい なんぼく	east, west, south and north

· · · ◇ · · ·

南アメリカ	みなみアメリカ	South America
南国	なんごく	southern provinces / country
南東の風	なんとうの かぜ	southeasterly wind
南極	なんきょく	South Pole, Antarctic

114 案 idea, plan, proposal

アン

丶 宀 宀 灾 安 安 安 宰
窜 案

案 combines 安 peaceful (cf. 233) and 木 tree. Under the peaceful shade of a tree, one may come up with a good idea. Associated meanings are plan and proposal.

案	あん	idea, plan, proposal
案内する	あんないする	to guide, to show
案内所	あんないじょ/しょ	information center
案内書	あんないしょ	guidebook
入学案内	にゅうがく あんない	guide to admission into school

· · · ◇ · · ·

原案	げんあん	original plan / bill
案内図	あんないず	guide / information map
名案	めいあん	good idea / proposal

115 便 convenience; mail

たよ・り、ベン、ビン

ノ イ 伝 仨 価 価 佰 便
便

更 depicts various things 品 put together in one 一 place by a hand 又. This makes them convenient for men 亻 to use. In the past, mail was the most convenient means of communication between people living far from each other.

便り	たより	letter, news
便所	べんじょ	lavatory
定期便	ていきびん	regular service flight / mail

· · · ◇ · · ·

便利な	べんりな	convenient
学内便	がくないびん	campus mail
船便	ふなびん	surface / sea mail
宅急便	たっきゅうびん	rapid door-to-door delivery

116 洗	wash あら・う、セン	、	ミ	シ	ジ	シ	汁	汼	洗
		洗							

洗 combines the radical 氵 water (cf. 28 水) and 先 toes (cf. 48). 洗 originally meant washing toes with water, and came to mean wash in general.

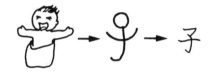

洗う	あらう	to wash
(お)手洗い	(お)てあらい	washroom, toilet
手洗所	てあらいじょ	washroom, toilet (formal)
洗面所	せんめんじょ	washroom, rest room
	・・・◇・・・	
洗濯機	せんたくき	washing machine
洗剤	せんざい	cleanser, detergent

117 子	child こ、シ	フ	フ	子					

子 depicts a baby in a bundle, indicating child.

子ども	こども	child
男の子	おとこのこ	boy
男子	だんし	boy, man, male
女子	じょし	girl, woman, female
	・・・◇・・・	
京子さん	きょうこさん	Kyoko-*san*
女子大	じょしだい	women's university / college
女子学生	じょし がくせい	female student

118 事	thing, affair; job こと、（ごと）、ジ	一	一	冖	口	弖	亨	事	事

事 depicts a hand holding a bamboo case containing fortunetelling sticks. A fortuneteller's job is to forecast various things.

事	こと	things, matter
火事	かじ	fire (destructive burning)
用事	ようじ	business, errand, things to do
工事中	こうじちゅう	under construction
	・・・◇・・・	
仕事	しごと	work, job
大事な	だいじな	important
事件	じけん	event, incident
返事する	へんじする	to answer, to reply

119 故	deceased, old; accidental	一	十	土	古	古	古	扩	故
	コ	故							

故 combines 十 ten, 口 mouth, and 攵, indicating an action (cf. 47 攻). 古 implies the act of oral transmission through some ten generations, meaning old. 故 thus means deceased as well as old. An associated meaning is accidental, because old things break down easily.

事故	じこ	accident
故障する	こしょうする	(for a machine, etc.) to break down, to become out of order

· · · ◇ · · ·

故人	こじん	the deceased
故郷	こきょう	hometown, native place

120 不	non-, un- (prefix)	一	フ	不	不				
	フ								

不 depicts a bird that has hit a ceiling and is not able to fly further up. 不 is generally used as a prefix like un- or non-.

不通	ふつう	interruption of traffic or telephone service
不便な	ふべんな	inconvenient

· · · ◇ · · ·

不用品	ふようひん	unnecessary / useless goods
不可	ふか	failure (in a school subject)
不足する	ふそくする	to be insufficient, to lack
不明な	ふめいな	unknown, obscure

4 PRACTICE

Ⅰ. Write the readings of the following kanji in hiragana.

1. 案 内 所   2. 男 子   3. 便 所   4. 女 子

5. お 手 洗 い   6. 手 洗 所   7. 事 故   8. 不 通

9. 故 障ᵇⁱᵍ (しょう)   10. 北 口   11. 南 口   12. 北 部

13. 東 南 アジア   14. 東 西 南 北   15. 入 学 案 内   16. 定 期 便

17. 洗 面 所   18. 男 の 子   19. 火 事   20. 不 便 な

21. わたしの 大学を 案内しました。

22. 母（はは）から 便りが ありません。 しんぱいです。

23. ごはんの 前に 手を 洗います。

24. 子どもは すぐ 大きくなります。

Ⅱ. Fill in the blanks with appropriate kanji.

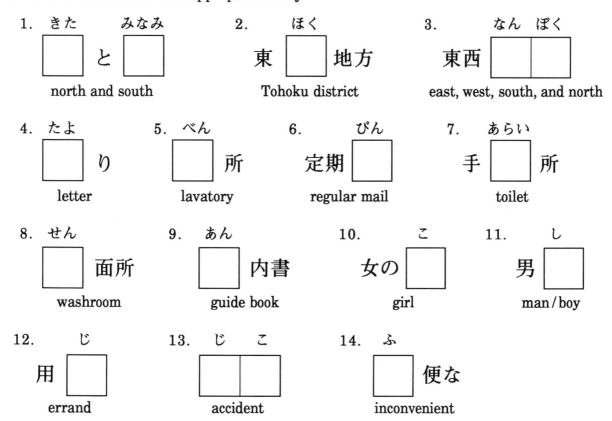

1. きた　みなみ
□ と □
north and south

2. ほく
東 □ 地方
Tohoku district

3. なん　ぼく
東西 □ □
east, west, south, and north

4. たよ
□ り
letter

5. べん
□ 所
lavatory

6. びん
定期 □
regular mail

7. あらい
手 □ 所
toilet

8. せん
□ 面所
washroom

9. あん
□ 内書
guide book

10. こ
女の □
girl

11. し
男 □
man / boy

12. じ
用 □
errand

13. じ　こ
□ □
accident

14. ふ
□ 便な
inconvenient

5 SUPPLEMENT

Some Signs Found in Stations

Shown on this page are some signs commonly found in stations. Check to see if they are familiar, and look for them in stations as well.

Out of Order

駅の ホーム

IF YOU have lived in Japan for some time, you probably have had the experience of taking the wrong train and wasting time and money. Most lines have local trains, semi-express trains, express trains, and special express trains. Maps posted inside the stations and trains show where each type of train stops. The sign in the upper photo shows departure times. The lower photo shows a platform at Shinjuku station, the busiest station in the world.

1 INTRODUCTORY QUIZ

Look at the illustration below and refer to the words in VOCABULARY. Then try the following quiz.

I. The guide below shows all the stops between terminal stations on a particular line. The various types of trains are marked with ○▲■◎ and labeled in kanji. Naturally, the fewer stops a train makes, the faster it goes. Fill in the spaces with the correct letters (a～g).

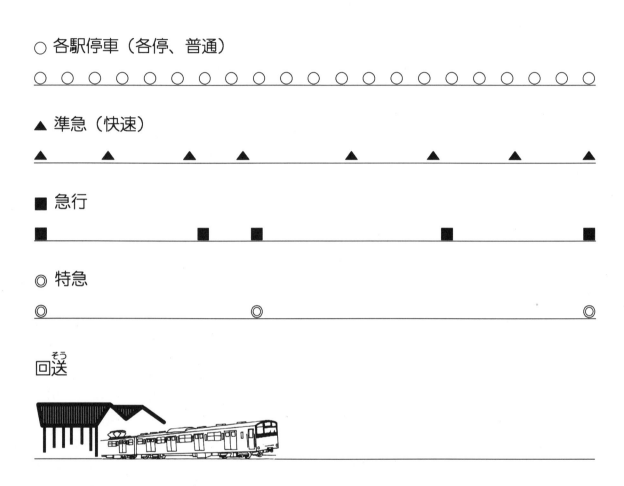

○ 各駅停車（各停、普通）

▲ 準急（快速）

■ 急行

◎ 特急

回送

1.（ ）と（ ）と（ ）は どの 駅にも とまります。
2.（ ）が 一番 はやいです。
3.（ ）には だれも のりません。
4.（ ）は 二番目に はやいです。
5.（ ）は 三番目に はやいです。

　　a. かくえきていしゃ　　b. とっきゅう　　c. じゅんきゅう　　d. きゅうこう
　　e. かくてい　　　　　　f. かいそう　　　g. ふつう

Ⅱ. Timetables for both weekdays and Sundays/holidays are found on the platforms. Shown below is part of a timetable for the Marunouchi Line. Read the timetable and fill in the spaces with the correct times.

発車時刻表

時	平日（新宿・荻窪
5	00 13 25 34 42 50 55
6	01 07 13 19 24 30 35 40 45 49 53 57
7	01 05 09 13 16 18 21 23 26 28 31 33 36 38
8	00 02 04 06 08 09 11 ~~13 15~~ ~~18 20~~ 22 24
	~~ ~~50~~ 58
21	03 09 14 19 24 29 34 39 44 49 54 59
22	04 09 14 19 24 30 34 39 44 49 56
23	02 07 16 25 31 38 46 55 **0** 02 17

時	休日（新宿・荻窪
5	03 13 25 35 45 54
6	02 10 16 22 28 34 39 46 52 58
7	04 10 16 22 28 34 39 45 50 56
8	01 07 12 ~~17~~ ~~24~~ 40 45 50 56
	~~ 12 16 21 29 37 45 ~~52 58~~
22	06 11 15 23 30 37 41 46 55
23	00 05 11 16 26 32 38 46 55
0	03

1. 水曜日の　始発は　（　　）時　（　　）分です。
2. 日曜日の　終発は　（　　）時　（　　）分です。

Ⅲ. This is part of a timetable for the Shinkansen Hikari ひかり and Kodama こだま trains. Along the top row from left to right is a list of trains. Along the left-hand column from top to bottom is a list of stations. Departure and arrival track numbers are also indicated. Choose the answers that correctly complete the statements on the next page.

列車名	◆ひかり322号	ひかり120号	ひかり90号	◆ひかり44号	◆ひかり44号	◆ひかり196号	ひかり140号	こだま458号	ひかり54号	こだま542号	ひかり20号	ひかり254号
発車番線				⑫		⑪	⑬		⑫	⑬	⑪	
博　多発	‥	‥	‥	1348	‥	1352	1358	‥	1405	1430	1435	‥
着	‥	‥	‥	1408	‥	1413	1418	‥	1425	1450	1455	‥
新神戸発	‥	‥	‥	1409	‥	1414	1419	‥	1426	1451	1456	‥
新大阪着	‥	‥	‥	1420	‥	1488	1450	‥	1500	1505	∨	‥
			1745	1737				‥	1741			
小田原発	∨	∨	∨	∨	∨			2107	∨	‥	∨	∨
新横浜着	∨	∨	2009	2002	2002		‥	2126	2109	‥	∨	∨
東　京着	1956	2008	2028	2020	2020	‥	‥	2144	2128	‥	2030	2036
到着番線	⑱	⑭	⑭	⑱	⑱			⑱	⑱	⑮	⑰	

1. ひかり322号は （ a. 東京へ　行きます。　b. 東京から　きます。）
2. ひかり90号は　東京（ a. 発　　b. 着 ）　20時　28分です。
3. ひかり20号の　発車番線は　（ a. 17　　b. 11 ）番線です。
4. この　時刻表は　（ a. 上り　　b. 下り ）の　新幹線の　時刻表です。

2 VOCABULARY

Study the readings and meanings of these words to help you understand the INTRODUC-TORY QUIZ.

1. 各駅停車	かく えき てい しゃ	local train
2. 各停	かく てい	local train (abbreviation for 各駅停車)
3. 普通	ふ つう	local train, slow train
4. 特急	とっ きゅう	special express
5. 回送	かい そう	out-of-service
6. 急行	きゅう こう	express train
7. 準急	じゅん きゅう	semi-express train
8. 快速	かい そく	semi-express train
9. 時刻表	じ こく ひょう	timetable
10. 始発	し はつ	the first train
11. 終発	しゅう はつ	the last train
12. ～号	～ ごう	train number ~
13. ～発	～ はつ	departure from/at ~
14. ～着	～ ちゃく	arrival at ~
15. 発車番線	はっ しゃ ばん せん	train departure track
16. 到着番線	とう ちゃく ばん せん	train arrival track
17. 上り	のぼ り	in-bound train
18. 下り	くだ り	out-bound train
19. 新幹線	しん かん せん	Shinkansen (bullet train)

3 NEW CHARACTERS

Twelve characters are introduced in this lesson. Use the explanations to help you understand and remember the characters. Study the compound words to increase your vocabulary.

各 停 普 準 急 速 快 特 表 終 着 発

121 各 each, every
カク、(カッ)

ノ ク タ 久 各 各

各 combines 久 trailing leg (cf. 22 後) and 口 here representing a square stone. When limping down a rocky road, one must stop and rest at every stone.

各地	かくち	each / every place, various places / districts
各自	かくじ	each person; respective
··· ◇ ···		
各位	かくい	Sirs (in a letter)
各国	かっこく	each / every country, various countries

122 停 stop, stay
テイ

ノ イ イ゛ 广 停 停 停 停
停 停 停

停 combines イ man, 高 immovable building, and 丁, which here represents an inserted nail and suggests remaining still. 停 thus implies people who stop or stay in one place.

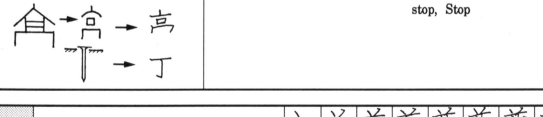

各駅停車	かくえき ていしゃ	local train
バス停	バスてい	bus stop
停留所	ていりゅうじょ	bus / streetcar stop
··· ◇ ···		
停電	ていでん	power failure
一時停止	いちじ ていし	temporary / momentary stop, Stop

123 普 general, ordinary
フ

丶 ソ 並 平 並 並 並 並
並 普 普 普

普 combines 並 and 日. 並 consists of two 立 stand (cf. 167), meaning side by side. Combined with 日, 普 implies that the sun's rays radiate out over a wide area. From this came the meaning of becoming widespread and eventually ordinary. By itself 並 also means ordinary.

普通	ふつう	ordinary, regular
普通電車	ふつう でんしゃ	local train
··· ◇ ···		
普通車	ふつうしゃ	ordinary-class car (train); ordinary-size car

124 準	level; semi-, sub- ジュン	丶	丷	シ	シ	汁	汁'	汁	汁
		浒	准	淮	淮	準			

準, which combines 氵water, 隹 fat bird (cf. 26 曜), and 十 many, suggests calm water where many birds gather. The surface of calm water is level.

$\cdots \diamond \cdots$

準備する	じゅんびする	to prepare
標準	ひょうじゅん	standard
水準	すいじゅん	level

---

125 急	hurry; urgent; sudden いそ・ぐ、キュウ	ノ	ク	⺈	刍	刍	刍	急	急
		急							

急 combines 刍, a hand reaching out to grab the man ahead, and 心, which derives from a pictograph of a heart and means mind. Together 急 means hurry or urgent.

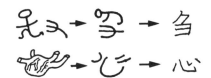

急ぐ	いそぐ	to hurry up
急行	きゅうこう	express train / bus
急用	きゅうよう	urgent business
準急	じゅんきゅう	semi-express train

$\cdots \diamond \cdots$

急停車する	きゅうていしゃする	to stop (car / train) suddenly
救急車	きゅうきゅうしゃ	ambulance
急行券	きゅうこうけん	express ticket

---

126 速	fast, quick, prompt はや・い、ソク	一	戸	戸	曰	束	束	束	束
		速	速						

速 combines 束 bundle tied in the middle and 辶 go (cf. 79 通). Carrying things in a bundle is faster than carrying them one by one.

速い	はやい	fast, rapid
時速	じそく	speed per hour

$\cdots \diamond \cdots$

速達	そくたつ	express mail
速度	そくど	speed, velocity

127 快 — pleasant, comfortable — カイ

Stroke order: ノ ハ 小 小ㄱ 忄ユ 快 快

快 combines 忄, a variation of 心 mind, and 夬, which means open because the left side is open compared with 央 (cf. 96). Opening the mind makes one feel pleasant.

心 → 小ㅣ → 忄

快速	かいそく	high speed, semi-express train
···◇···		
快晴	かいせい	clear and beautiful weather
全快する	ぜんかいする	to recover completely from an illness

128 特 — special — トク、(トッ)

Stroke order: ノ ト 牛 牛 牜 牛 牜 牛 特 特

特 combines 牜, which is a variation of 牛 cow (cf. 227), a typical slow-moving animal, and 寺 move hands and feet (cf. 23 時). 特 thus indicates a cow moving quickly, which makes it special.

特に	とくに	in particular, especially
特急	とっきゅう	special express train / bus
···◇···		
特別な	とくべつな	special
特長	とくちょう	strong point, merit
特徴	とくちょう	characteristic, peculiarity
特急券	とっきゅうけん	special express ticket

129 表 — surface, front; list, table; expression — おもて、ヒョウ、(ピョウ)

Stroke order: 一 十 キ 主 표 表 表 表

表 combines 毛 hair or fur and 衣 clothes. A fur coat is an outer garment; thus 表 means surface. The surface of a thing can also express something about its content. An example of this is a list.

毛 → 主 / 衣

表	おもて	the surface / front
表-4	ひょう-よん	Table 4
時間表	じかんひょう	schedule (of classes, work), timetable
···◇···		
表面	ひょうめん	surface
表紙	ひょうし	front cover of a book
時刻表	じこくひょう	schedule (of trains), timetable
代表する	だいひょうする	to represent

111

130 終	end, come to an end	く 乆 幺 糸 糸 糸 糸 終
	お・わる、シュウ	紣 終 終

糸 thread (cf. 85 線) suggests closing a bag by tying it. 冬 depicts foods being hung over ice to store for the winter, the season that ends the year. The two characters together make 終, meaning end.

終（わ）る	おわる	to end, to be finished
終電	しゅうでん	last train
	. . . ◇ . . .	
終日	しゅうじつ	all day long
終点	しゅうてん	last stop, rail terminal
終了する	しゅうりょうする	to be closed, to be completed

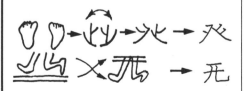

131 着	arrive; wear, dress	丶 ヽゝ ュ ゼ 羊 羊 羊
	つ・く、き・る、（ぎ）、チャク	羊 着 着 着

着 combines 芊, which derives from 羊 sheep, and 目 eye. Sheep are easily seen when they arrive. Thus 着 means arrive. Associated meanings are attach and wear.

着く	つく	to arrive
着る	きる	to put on clothes
上着	うわぎ	coat, jacket
五時着	ごじちゃく	five o'clock arrival
	. . . ◇ . . .	
着物	きもの	Japanese clothes, kimono
下着	したぎ	underwear
終着駅	しゅうちゃくえき	terminal station
発着時間	はっちゃく じかん	departure and arrival times

132 発	leave, depart; emit	フ フ フ゜ 癶 癶 癶 癶 発
	ハツ、（ハッ）、（パツ）	発

発 combines 癶, depicting outspread feet ready to start walking, and 兀, indicating legs about to leave a starting line. Thus 発 has come to mean leave or depart.

五時発	ごじはつ	five o'clock departure
始発	しはつ	the first train / bus
終発	しゅうはつ	the last train / bus
発車する	はっしゃする	to depart (train / car)
出発する	しゅっぱつする	to start / depart
	. . . ◇ . . .	
発音する	はつおんする	to pronounce
発電所	はつでんしょ	power plant
発表する	はっぴょうする	to announce, to make a presentation

4 PRACTICE

Ⅰ. Write the readings of the follwing kanji in hiragana.

1. 各駅停車　2. 普通　　3. 特急　　4. 回送（そう）　5. 急行

6. 準急　　　7. 快速　　8. 時刻（こく）表　9. 始発　10. 終発

11. ～号　　　12. ～発　　13. ～着　　14. 発車番線

15. 新幹（かん）線　16. 停留所　17. 急用　18. 時速　19. 特に

20. 時間表　　21. 出発

22. きっぷは　各自で　かってください。

23. 電車が　きます。急いでください。

24. もう　しごとは　終わりました。

25. 十時に　東京駅に　着きました。

26. さむいですね。上着を　着て　出かけましょう。

Ⅱ. Fill in the blanks with appropriate kanji.

1. ふ	2. じゅんきゅう	3. きゅう	4. てい

1. ふ
☐ 通電車
local train

2. じゅんきゅう
☐☐
semi-express train

3. きゅう
☐ 用
urgent business

4. てい
☐ 車駅
station to stop at

5. かく　てい
☐☐
local train

6. とく　はや

especially fast

7. かい　そく
☐☐
semi-express train

8. おもて
☐
the surface

9. ひょう
☐ ― 4
Table 4

10. お
☐ わる
to end

11. しゅう
☐ 電
the last train

12. つ
☐ く
to arrive

13. ちゃく
五時 ☐
5:00 arrival

14. はつ
四時 ☐
4:00 departure

15. はっ
☐ 車する
to depart

16. ぱつ
出 ☐ する
to depart

REVIEW EXERCISE   Lessons 6–10

I. Find kanji having common radicals or elements, and write them or their corresponding letters in the blanks.

1. 後: ☐   2. 回: ☐   3. 定: ☐   4. 洗: ☐

5. 金: ☐   6. 学: ☐   7. 込: ☐ ☐

8. 終: ☐ ☐   9. 使: ☐ ☐ ☐ ☐

a. 行	b. 鉄	c. 営	d. 人	e. 準
f. 線	g. 停	h. 団	i. 連	j. 案
k. 絡	l. 便	m. 代	n. 速	

10. 時: ☐   11. 留: ☐   12. 内: ☐   13. 攻: ☐   14. 所: ☐

| o. 新 | p. 都 | q. 故 | r. 番 | s. 特 | t. 央 |

II. Find the antonyms to the kanji below, and write them or their corresponding letters in the blanks.

1. 大 ↔ ☐   5. 南 ↔ ☐

2. 入 ↔ ☐   6. 始 ↔ ☐

3. 上 ↔ ☐   7. 発 ↔ ☐

4. 東 ↔ ☐

a. 青   b. 西   c. 出   d. 央   e. 小   f. 午   g. 終   h. 人   i. 下   j. 北   k. 中

銀 行

ALL BANKS in Japan have automatic teller machines (ATMs). Once you have opened an account and had a cash card with a secret code number made, you can withdraw or deposit money at any branch or affiliated bank. Becoming familiar with the kanji at ATMs will help you use any type of machine. Banks are usually open from 9:00 a.m. to 3:00 or 4:00 p.m. Monday through Friday, but ATMs continue to operate until 6:00 or 7:00 p.m. Withdrawals can be made on Saturdays as well, and at some branches even on Sundays. ATMs are conveniently located in such places as department stores, large stations, and shopping streets.

1 INTRODUCTORY QUIZ

Look at the illustrations below and refer to the words in VOCABULARY. Then try the following quiz.

Mr. Lee is at the bank with his cash card and bankbook. He wants to use the ATM but doesn't know the meaning of the kanji displayed on the machine. Therefore he asks a bank employee for assistance.

Ⅰ. Read the dialogue below and write (a) or (b) in the spaces provided.

a   b

 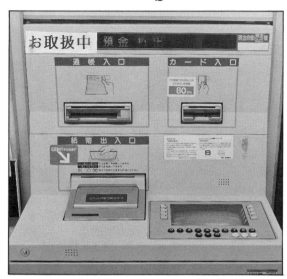

リー　　：「すみません。　いま、どちらのきかいを使ったらいいですか。」

銀行の人：「＿＿＿＿のきかいを使ってください。　＿＿＿＿のきかいは使えません。」

Here are some key words to know when using an ATM.

押す   入れる   取る

 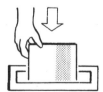 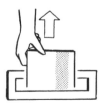

Ⅱ. While reading the following dialogue, look at the kanji on the ATM screen below and write the correct letters (A~F) in the spaces provided.

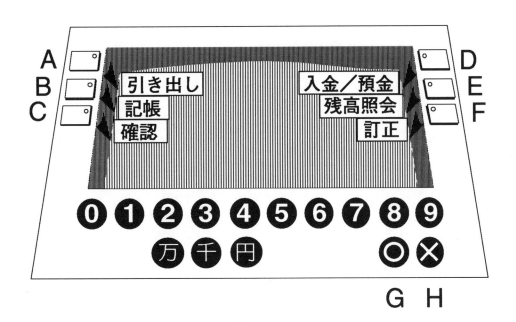

1. リー　　　：「お金を預けたいんですが、どのボタンを押すんですか。」
　　銀行の人：「はじめに、＿＿＿＿のボタンを押してください。　それから、通帳とお金を
　　　　　　　入れてください。」

2. リー　　　：「25,000円、引き出したいんですが・・・・・。」
　　銀行の人：「はじめに、＿＿＿＿のボタンを押してください。それから、カードを入れて、
　　　　　　　暗証番号を押します。つぎに、2・万・5・千・円のボタンを押して、正し
　　　　　　　かったら、＿G＿か＿＿＿＿のボタンを押してください。」

3. リー　　　：「あっ、暗証番号をまちがえた！　どうしたらいいですか。」
　　銀行の人：「＿H＿か＿＿＿＿のボタンを押してください。」

4. リー　　　：「いま、お金がいくら残っているか、みたいんですが・・・・・。」
　　銀行の人：「＿＿＿＿のボタンを押して、カードを入れて、暗証番号を押してくだい。」

5. リー　　　：「お金がいくらあるか通帳に記入したいんですが・・・・・。」
　　銀行の人：「＿＿＿＿のボタンを押して、通帳を入れてください。」

2 VOCABULARY

Study the readings and meanings of these words to help you understand the INTRODUCTORY QUIZ.

1.	銀行	ぎん こう	bank
2.	休止	きゅう し	out of use
3.	(お)取扱中	（お）とり あつかい ちゅう	available for use
4.	きかい		machine
5.	使う	つか う	to use
6.	押す	お す	to push
7.	入れる	い れる	to put in
8.	取る	と る	to take out
9.	ボタン		button
10.	引き出し	ひ き だし	withdrawal
11.	入金／預金	にゅう きん／よ きん	deposit
12.	記帳	き ちょう	entry in a bank book
13.	残高照会	ざん だか しょう かい	checking the balance
14.	確認	かく にん	confirmation
15.	訂正	てい せい	correction
16.	預ける	あず ける	to deposit
17.	通帳	つう ちょう	bankbook
18.	暗証番号	あん しょう ばん ごう	secret code number
19.	正しい	ただ しい	correct
20.	まちがえる		to make a mistake
21.	残る	のこ る	to remain
22.	記入する	き にゅう する	to make an entry

3 NEW CHARACTERS

Eighteen characters are introduced in this lesson. Use the explanations to help you understand and remember the characters. Study the compound words to increase your vocabulary.

銀 引 預 押 号 暗 証 確 認 訂 正 残 高 記
帳 取 扱 止

133 銀	silver	ノ	八	스	仐	仐	牟	余	金
	ギン	金ㄱ	金ㅋ	金ㅋ	釾	鉅	銀		

銀 combines 金 metal (cf. 30) and 艮 white root or white ground. White metal from the ground is silver. Another explanation is that 艮 is like 良 good (cf. 180 食) without '. Metal that is not as good as gold 金 is silver 銀.

銀	ぎん	silver
銀行	ぎんこう	bank
・・・◇・・・		
銀×座	ぎんざ	Ginza (place)
銀メダル	ぎんメダル	silver medal
水銀	すいぎん	mercury

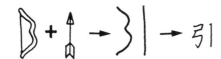

白 + → 泉 → 艮

---

134 引	pull, draw; reduce	フ	コ	弓	引				
	ひ・く、(び・き)、イン								

引 derives from a pictograph of a bow and arrow. When shooting, the arrow is pulled back before it's let go.

引く	ひく	to pull
引(き)出す	ひきだす	to pull ~ out; to withdraw money
引(き)出(し)	ひきだし	drawer; withdrawal (from bank account)
・・・◇・・・		
百円引(き)	ひゃくえん びき	one hundred yen discount
引×力	いんりょく	gravity

◇ + ↟ → ⻋ → 引

---

135 預	receive/entrust for safekeeping	フ	マ	孓	予	予	予	予	預
	あず・かる、あず・ける、ヨ	預	預	預	預	預			

預 combines 予 in advance (cf. 243) and 頁 head or person. Preparing for something in advance allows people to feel safe. Thus 預 means entrust to or receive from someone for safekeeping.

預かる	あずかる	to be entrusted with ~
預(け)入れ	あずけいれ	depositing
預ける	あずける	to leave ~ in someone's care; to deposit
預金する	よきんする	to deposit money
・・・◇・・・		
一時預(か)り所	いちじ あずかりしょ	checkroom, temporary storage
定期預金	ていき よきん	fixed deposit
普通預金	ふつう よきん	ordinary deposit

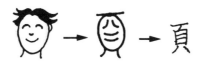

→ → 頁

136 押 push, press
お・す

一 十 扌 扣 扣 扣 押 押

押 combines 扌 hand (cf. 88 手) and 甲, representing both a turtle's shell and the back of a hand because of their similar shapes. Thus 押 means push because when pushing something, one sees the back of one's hand.

押す	おす	to push, to press
· · · ◇ · · ·		
押(し)入(れ)	おしいれ	closet

---

137 号 number
ゴウ

丶 口 口 吕 号

号 depicts a mouth shouting. In physical education class, students line up and shout out their numbers in order. Thus 号 means number when it shows the order of something.

番号	ばんごう	number (showing an order)
六号車	ろくごうしゃ	car no. 6
· · · ◇ · · ·		
年号	ねんごう	name of an era
信号	しんごう	signal
七月号	しちがつごう	July issue (magazine)

---

138 暗 dark, unseen
くら・い、アン

丨 冂 日 日 日' 日立 日立 日立
暗 暗 暗 暗 暗

暗 combines 日 sun and 音, which is formed by adding a bar 一 to 口 of 言 say (cf. 78 話) and suggests confining someone's voice by covering his mouth. If the sun is covered, it becomes dark. By itself 音 means sound.

暗い	くらい	dark
· · · ◇ · · ·		
暗号	あんごう	cipher, secret code
暗室	あんしつ	photography darkroom

139 証	proof, certificate ショウ	、	二	亠	言	言	言	言	訂
		訂	訂	訂	証				

証, which combines 言 say and 正 correct (cf. 143), suggests saying something correct. This has come to mean proof or certificate.

暗証番号　あんしょう ばんごう　secret code number
学生証　　がくせいしょう　　　student ID card
　　　　　　・・・ ◇ ・・・
保証する　ほしょうする　　　　to guarantee

140 確	ascertain, make sure たし・かめる、カク	一	ア	イ	石	石	石	石	矿
		矿	矿	矿	碓	碓	確	確	

確 combines 石 stone, 宀 house, and 隹 bird (cf. 26 曜). If birds hide in a stone house, they can be sure of their safety.

確かめる　たしかめる　　　　to make sure, to confirm
　　　　　　・・・ ◇ ・・・
確実な　　かくじつな　　　　sure, certain
正確な　　せいかくな　　　　accurate, exact

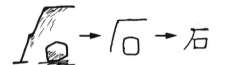

141 認	recognize, approve みと・める、ニン	、	二	亠	言	言	言	言	訂
		訒	訒	訒	認	認	認		

忍, which combines 刃 blade (cf. 61 券) and 心 mind (cf. 125 急), means bearing pain. With the addition of 言 words, 認 formerly meant bearing sharp words, and eventually came to mean recognize or approve.

認める　　みとめる　　　　　to recognize, to approve
確認する　かくにんする　　　to confirm, to make sure
　　　　　　・・・ ◇ ・・・
認定する　にんていする　　　to approve, to certify
公認する　こうにんする　　　to approve / recognize
　　　　　　　　　　　　　officially

142 訂　correct　テイ

、	二	三	言	言	言	言	言
訂							

訂 combines 言 words and 丁 nail hammered into a board at a right angle (cf. 122 停). Thus 訂 means righting or correcting what has been written or spoken.

・・・◇・・・

改訂する　かいていする　to revise

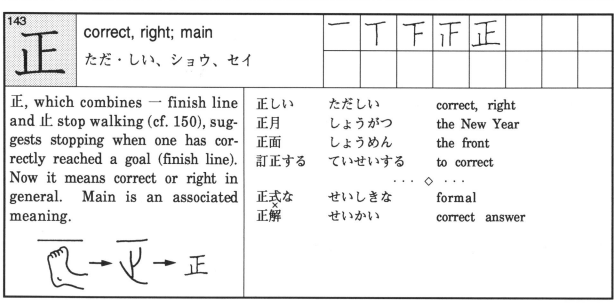

143 正　correct, right; main　ただ・しい、ショウ、セイ

一	丁	F	正	正			

正, which combines 一 finish line and 止 stop walking (cf. 150), suggests stopping when one has correctly reached a goal (finish line). Now it means correct or right in general.　Main is an associated meaning.

正しい	ただしい	correct, right
正月	しょうがつ	the New Year
正面	しょうめん	the front
訂正する	ていせいする	to correct

・・・◇・・・

正式な	せいしきな	formal
正解	せいかい	correct answer

144 残　remain, left behind　のこ・る、のこ・す、ザン

一	丁	歹	歹	歹	歹	歹	残
残	残						

残, which combines 歹 bone and 戔 two weapons (cf. 33 成), represents bones left after the meat has been taken off with weapons. Thus 残 means left behind or remain.

残る	のこる	to be left over, to remain; to stay
残金	ざんきん	money left over, bank account balance

・・・◇・・・

残す	のこす	to leave
残業する	ざんぎょうする	to work overtime
残暑	ざんしょ	late summer heat
残念な	ざんねんな	unfortunate, regrettable

145 高 high; expensive
たか・い、(だか)、コウ

一	二	六	古	古	占	高	高
高	高						

高 depicts a two storied house, which was considered high in ancient times. An associated meaning is high price, or expensive.

高い	たかい	high; expensive
円高	えんだか	high value of the yen
残高	ざんだか	bank account balance

· · · ◇ · · ·

高気圧	こうきあつ	high atmospheric pressure
高校	こうこう	high school

146 記 take note, write
キ

丶	二	二	言	言	言	言	記
記	記						

己 suggests that something lying down has risen up and become noticeable. Together with 言 words, 記 implies words to note, and thus means take note or write.

記入する	きにゅうする	to make an entry, to fill out / in
日記	にっき	diary
記号	きごう	mark, sign, symbol
暗記する	あんきする	to learn by heart, to memorize

· · · ◇ · · ·

記事	きじ	news story, article
記念日	きねんび	memorial day, anniversary
新聞記者	しんぶん きしゃ	newspaper reporter

147 帳 notebook
チョウ

一	口	巾	巾	巾	巾	巾	帳
帳	帳	帳					

帳 combines 巾 hanging cloth, and 長 long, which originally depicted an old man with long hair leaning on a cane. A long cloth was used as a notebook in ancient times.

記帳する	きちょうする	to make an entry in a bankbook; to sign a visitors' register
通帳	つうちょう	bankbook
手帳	てちょう	small notebook, datebook
電話帳	でんわちょう	telephone directory

· · · ◇ · · ·

148 取　take, get, acquire
と・る、（ど・り）

一　丁　下　下　耳　耳　取　取

取 combines 耳 ear and 又 hand. Ancient warriors used to take the ears off their conquered enemies. Now 取 means take or get in general.

取る	とる	to take, to get
取（り）引（き）する	とりひきする	to trade, to make a deal
取（り）出す	とりだす	to take out, to pick out
間取（り）	まどり	room arrangement of a house, floor plan
・・・◇・・・		
取（り）消（し）	とりけし	cancellation

149 扱　treat, deal with, handle
あつか・う

一　扌　扌　扔　扱　扱

扱 combines 扌 hand (cf. 88 手) and 及 another hand reaching out for a man. Only when hands reach something, can one treat or handle it.

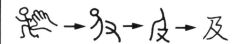

扱う	あつかう	to treat, to handle, to deal with
取（り）扱（い）中	とりあつかいちゅう	under handling; Available for Use
扱い方	あつかいかた	how to handle / treat / use, way of handling
・・・◇・・・		

150 止　stop
と・まる、（ど・まり）、と・める、（ど・め）、シ

丨　ト　𣥂　止

止 derives from a pictograph of a foot that has stopped walking. Other kanji including 止 are often related to walking (e.g. 143 正, 164 歩).

止（ま）る	とまる	to stop (vi.)
行（き）止（ま）り	いきどまり	Dead End
止める	とめる	to stop (vt.)
通行止（め）	つうこうどめ	Closed to Traffic
休止する	きゅうしする	to discontinue, to halt
・・・◇・・・		
止まれ	とまれ	Stop
中止する	ちゅうしする	to stop (vt.), to cancel

4 PRACTICE

I. Write the readings of the following kanji in hiragana.

1. 銀 行　2. 休 止　3. 高 い　4. 十 号 車　5. 引 き 出 し

6. 入 金　7. 預 金　8. 確 認　9. 預 け る　10. 暗 証 番 号

11. 訂 正　12. 記 号　13. 記 帳　14. 学 生 証　15. お 取 扱 中

16. 取 る　17. 暗 い　18. 引 く　19. 電 話 帳　20. 通 行 止 め

21. 円 高　22. 正 月　23. 残 高　24. 扱 い 方

25. ベルを押してください。　　　26. 正しいほうに、○をつけなさい。

27. いつも、日記を書いています。

28. 通帳に、記入してください。

29. いくらお金が残っているか、確かめてみます。

30. 手をあげて、タクシーを止めます。

II. Fill in the blanks with appropriate kanji.

1. ぎん	2. ひ	3. あず	4. よ
□ 行	□ き出す	□ け入れ	□ 金する
bank	to withdraw	depositing	to deposit money

5. お	6. かく にん	7. しょう	8. くら
□ す	□□ する	学生 □	□ い
to push	to confirm	student ID card	dark

9. あん しょう ごう	10. のこ	11. ざん	12. ちょう
□□ 番 □	□ る	□ 金	手 □
secret code number	to remain	money left over	small notebook

13. き ごう	14. しょう	15. てい せい	16. たか
□□	□ 面	□□ する	□ い
mark	the front	to correct	high

17. ざん だか
□□
the balance

18. あつか
□う
to treat

19. と
□り出す
to take out

20. と
□まる
to stop

21. し
休□
out of use

---

5 SUPPLEMENT

Charges for utilities such as electricity, gas, water, and telephone can be paid automatically from an account.

Form to Apply for Automatic Payment

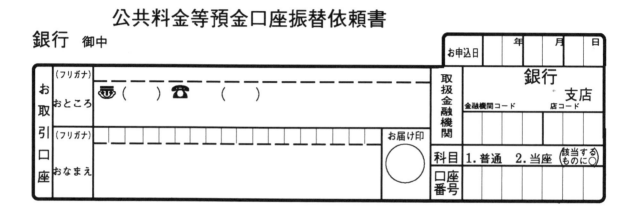

Receipt for Automatic Payment (sent directly to consumer)

Electricity　　　　　　　　　　　**Gas**

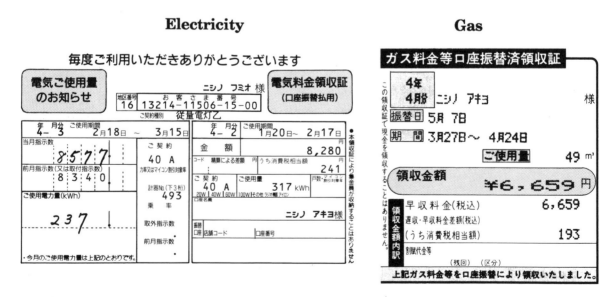

郵便局

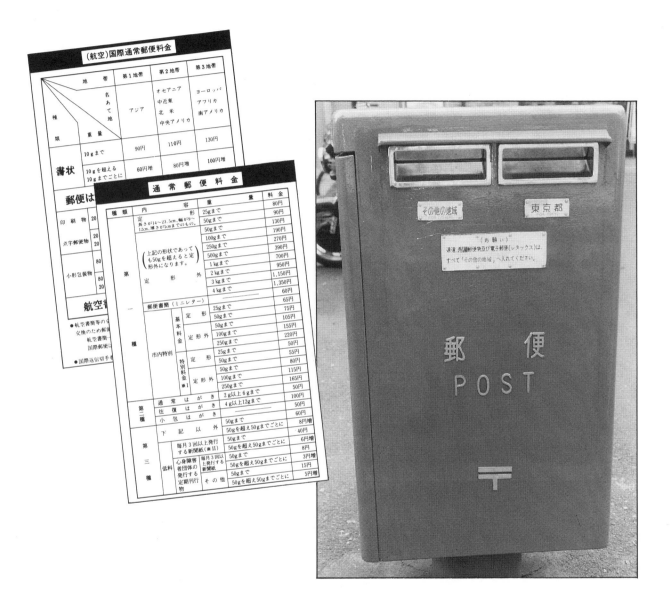

BUILDINGS MARKED with 〒 are post offices. Inside are several windows, not only for the usual postal services, but also for savings accounts, money transfers, and other banking services. The window marked with はがき・切手 is where stamps, postcards, and aerogrammes can be bought. Stamps are also sold at any shop marked with 〒. For people who are unsure of the stamp value needed for their mail, lists of postal rates are available at post offices. City post boxes have two letter drops, with mailing instructions written below them.

1 INTRODUCTORY QUIZ

Look at the illustrations below and refer to the words in VOCABULARY. Then try the following quiz.

Ⅰ. Refer to the lists of postal rates on the next page and write the appropriate rates for each piece of mail in the spaces provided below. None of the letters exceeds 10g. A ¥80 stamp is already attached to (e), so fill in only the express delivery rate.

a:_____ b:_____ c:_____ d:_____ e:_____

a
Mr. I. Ronson

Lagos, <u>NIGERIA</u>

VIA AIR MAIL

b
Ryoan-ji Temple, Rock Garden, Kyoto

POST CARD

おげんきですか。
日本はもう春です。さくら
のはながさいています。
ことしも日本からヒマラヤに
のぼる人が何人も行くという
ニュースをききました。
また おあいするのを たのし
みにしています。
さようなら

Mr. M. R. Rimel
Katmandu
Nepal

AIR MAIL

c
Mr. M. Smith
Washington D.C.
<u>U.S.A.</u>

VIA AIR MAIL

d
郵便はがき
169-□□

東京都大田区百人町
二一四一六
山田正子様

e
341-□□

埼玉県三郷市彦成一二一一〇一
ヤン・リー様
—速達—

郵便料金表 (Postal Rates)

国際

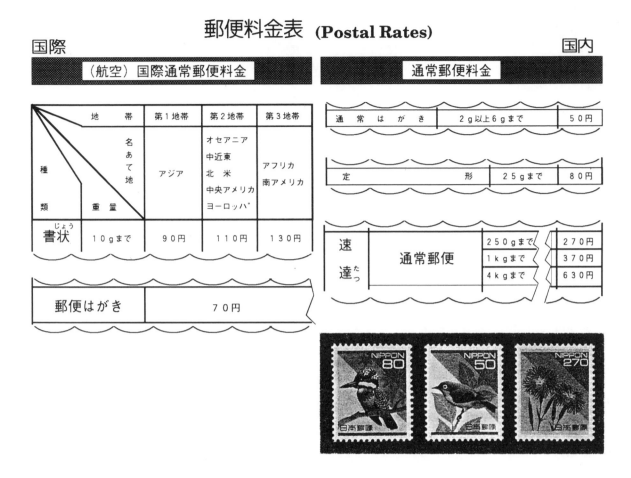

国内

（航空）国際通常郵便料金

地　帯 種　類　重　量	第1地帯 名あて地 アジア	第2地帯 オセアニア 中近東 北　米 中央アメリカ ヨーロッパ	第3地帯 アフリカ 南アメリカ
書状(じょう) 10gまで	90円	110円	130円

郵便はがき	70円

通常郵便料金

通常はがき	2g以上6gまで	50円

定　　　　　　形	25gまで	80円

速達(たっ)	通常郵便	250gまで	270円
		1kgまで	370円
		4kgまで	630円

Ⅱ. Now mail the letters and postcards from the previous page, choosing the correct letter drop 1 or 2. Read the instructions below the letter drops and write the letters (a～e) corresponding to the pieces of mail in the spaces provided.

　　　　1.(　　　　　　　　　　)　　2.(　　　　　　　　　　)

2 VOCABULARY

Study the readings and meanings of these words to help you understand the INTRODUC-TORY QUIZ.

1. 郵便局 　ゆう びん きょく　　post office
2. はがき　　　　　　　　　　postcard
3. 切手　　きって　　　　　　postage stamp
4. 航空(便)　こう くう（びん）　airmail
5. 国際　　こく さい　　　　　international
6. 通常　　つう じょう　　　　ordinary
7. 郵便料金　ゆう びん りょう きん　postal rate
8. アジア　　　　　　　　　　Asia
9. 北米　　ほく べい　　　　　North America
10. アフリカ　　　　　　　　　Africa
11. 書状／手紙　しょ じょう／て がみ　letter
12. 定形　　てい けい　　　　　standard size (envelope)
13. 速達　　そく たつ　　　　　express mail
14. その他の地域　その た の ち いき　other areas
15. お願い　　お ねが い　　　　request (notice)
16. 外国郵便　がい こく ゆう びん　overseas mail
17. 電子郵便　でん し ゆう びん　electronic mail using facsimile
18. ～様　　～ さま　　　　　　Mr. ~, Ms. ~, Miss ~, Mrs. ~
19. 右側　　みぎ がわ　　　　　right side
20. 差入れ口　さし いれ ぐち　　letter drop

3 NEW CHARACTERS

Twelve characters are introduced in this lesson. Use the explanations to help you understand and remember the characters. Study the compound words to increase your vocabulary.

郵 局 切 外 国 際 航 空 常 料 他 様

151 郵	mail ユウ	ノ	ニ	二	千	弁	岙	垂	垂
		郵	郵						

垂 depicts a plant with leaves hanging vertically; vertical also refers to vertical cliffs far away. With the addition of ß village, 郵 formerly meant outposts for the relay of messages, and eventually came to mean mail.

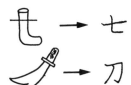

郵便	ゆうびん	mail service
郵便番号	ゆうびん ばんごう	postal / zip code
	・・・◇・・・	
郵送料	ゆうそうりょう	postage
郵便物	ゆうびんぶつ	mail

---

152 局	bureau, office キョク	フ	コ	尸	局	局	局	局

局 combines 尹 enclose with two bent lines (as shown below), and 口 limited or divided space. Offices are enclosed spaces that are divided into sections.

郵便局	ゆうびんきょく	post office
電話局	でんわきょく	telephone office
局番	きょくばん	district telephone number
	・・・◇・・・	
テレビ局	テレビきょく	television station

---

153 切	cut き・る、（きっ）、（ぎっ）、セツ	一	七	切	切

切, which combines 七 branch being cut, and 刀 sword (cf. 25 分), means cut.

切る	きる	to cut
切手	きって	postage stamp
小切手	こぎって	check
大切な	たいせつな	important, valuable
	・・・◇・・・	
締(め)切(り)	しめきり	deadline
切符	きっぷ	ticket
親切な	しんせつな	kind

154 外	outside; other	ノ	ク	タ	タト	外			
	そと、ガイ、ゲ								

外 combines 夕 evening (cf. 66 名) and 卜, which depicts a stick used by fortunetellers. In ancient China, fortunetellers worked outside in the evening.

外	そと	outside
外出する	がいしゅつする	to go out
時間外	じかんがい	before or after office / working hours; overtime
外科	げか	surgical unit, surgery
	・・・◇・・・	
外側	そとがわ	outside
外来	がいらい	coming from outside; for an outpatient
海外	かいがい	overseas
内外	ないがい	inside and outside

155 国	country, nation	丨	冂	冂	冂	国	国	国	
	くに、コク、（ゴク）、（コッ）								

王 represents a man standing between heaven and earth with hands and legs spread wide, indicating a king. 丶 suggests treasure. A king and his treasures enclosed by borders 囗 represents country.

国	くに	country, nation
外国	がいこく	foreign country
外国人	がいこくじん	foreigner
中国	ちゅうごく	China
	・・・◇・・・	
四国	しこく	Shikoku (island, district)
国籍	こくせき	nationality
国内	こくない	domestic, within the country
国会	こっかい	the Diet

156 際	inter-; occasion	⁊	阝	阝	阝	阝	阝	阝	阝⁊
	サイ	阝ｽ	阝欠	際	際	際	際		

際 combines 阝, which as a left part of kanji means piled stones or hill, and 祭 festival (cf. 36). Festivals held on hills used to be important occasions during which people intermingled.

国際	こくさい	international
国際線	こくさいせん	international flight / route
国際電話	こくさい でんわ	international phone call
	・・・◇・・・	
国際交流	こくさい こうりゅう	international exchange
この際	このさい	on this occasion

157 航	navigation, sailing コウ	ノ	⺈	丹	丹	舟	舟	舟`	舟亠
		舟`	航						

舟 derives from a pictograph of a boat, and 亢 represents a neck held up straight. Thus 航 means sailing straight forward.

日航	にっこう	abbreviation for 日本航空 (Japan Air Lines)
	・・・ ◇ ・・・	
航海する	こうかいする	to navigate, to sail, to voyage

---

158 空	sky; empty, vacant そら、から、あ・く、クウ	`	⺌	宀	宀	穴	空	空	空

穴 or 宂, which combines 宀 house and 八 divide (cf. 8), formerly meant pit or cave dwelling, and now means hole in general. 工 indicates straight (cf. 47 攻). The sky can be thought of as a large hole where one can go straight up and find nothing but emptiness.

空	そら	sky
空手	からて	karate
航空便	こうくうびん	airmail
空車	くうしゃ	vacant taxi
	・・・ ◇ ・・・	
空オケ	からオケ	karaoke (literally "empty orchestra")
空きカン	あきカン	empty can
成田空港	なりた くうこう	Narita Airport
空席	くうせき	vacant / unoccupied seat

---

159 常	always, normal, usual ジョウ	`	⺌	⺌	씨	쓰	常	常	常
		常	常	常					

常 combines 尚 long wisps of smoke coming out of a stove, and 巾 cloth (cf. 147 帳). Long cloth eventually came to mean long time, and now 常 means always or normal.

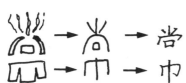

通常	つうじょう	usually, normally, in general
平常通り	へいじょう どおり	as usual
正常な	せいじょうな	normal
	・・・ ◇ ・・・	
日常会話	にちじょう かいわ	daily conversation
非常の際	ひじょうの さい	in case of emergency
非常階段	ひじょう かいだん	emergency stairs

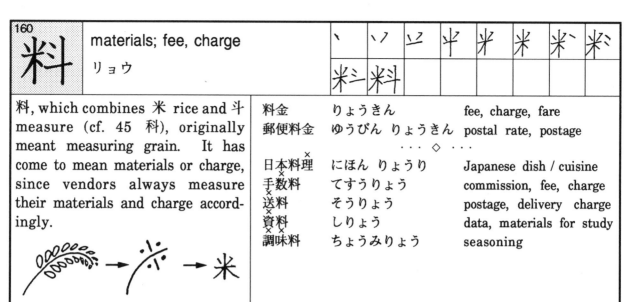

160 料	materials; fee, charge リョウ	、	丷	丷	半	半	米	米	米
		米ニ	料						

料, which combines 米 rice and 斗 measure (cf. 45 科), originally meant measuring grain. It has come to mean materials or charge, since vendors always measure their materials and charge accordingly.

料金	りょうきん	fee, charge, fare
郵便料金	ゆうびん りょうきん	postal rate, postage
・・・◇・・・		
日本料理	にほん りょうり	Japanese dish / cuisine
手数料	てすうりょう	commission, fee, charge
送料	そうりょう	postage, delivery charge
資料	しりょう	data, materials for study
調味料	ちょうみりょう	seasoning

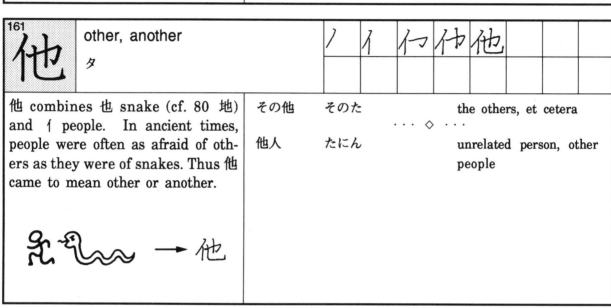

161 他	other, another タ	ノ	イ	イ⁻	忄	他		

他 combines 也 snake (cf. 80 地) and 亻 people. In ancient times, people were often as afraid of others as they were of snakes. Thus 他 came to mean other or another.

その他	そのた	the others, et cetera
・・・◇・・・		
他人	たにん	unrelated person, other people

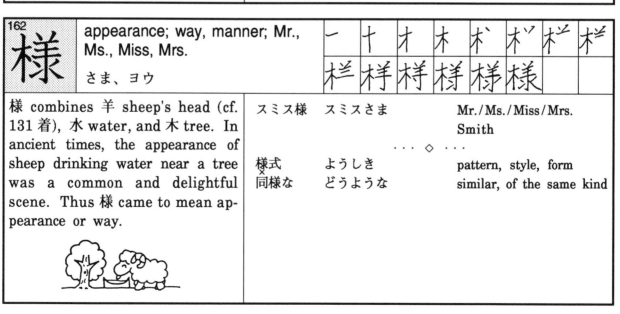

162 様	appearance; way, manner; Mr., Ms., Miss, Mrs. さま、ヨウ	一	十	才	木	栏	栏	栏	栏
		栏	样	样	様	様	様		

様 combines 羊 sheep's head (cf. 131 着), 水 water, and 木 tree. In ancient times, the appearance of sheep drinking water near a tree was a common and delightful scene. Thus 様 came to mean appearance or way.

スミス様	スミスさま	Mr. / Ms. / Miss / Mrs. Smith
・・・◇・・・		
様式	ようしき	pattern, style, form
同様な	どうような	similar, of the same kind

4 PRACTICE

Ⅰ. Write the readings of the following kanji in hiragana.

1. 郵 便 局　　　2. 切 手　　　3. 航 空 便　　　4. 国 際

5. 通 常　　　6. 料 金　　　7. 書 状(じょう)　　　8. 定 形(けい)

9. 速 達(たつ)　　　10. そ の 他　　　11. 外 国　　　12. 〜 様

13. 郵 便 番 号　　14. 電 話 局　　15. 小 切 手　　16. 時 間 外

17. 外 科　　　18. 国 際 線　　19. 中 国　　　20. 空 車

21. 大切なご本、ありがとうございました。

22. 子どもが、外でげんきにあそんでいます。

23. 国から便りがありました。

24. スミスさんは、外国人ですが、空手がじょうずです。

25. あしたも平常通り扱います。

Ⅱ. Fill in the blanks with appropriate kanji.

1. ゆう　きょく
□ 便 □
post office

2. きょく
□ 番
district phone number

3. き
□ る
to cut

4. きっ
□ 手
postage stamp

5. そと
□
outside

6. くに
いろいろな □
various countries

7. がい　こく
□ □ 便
overseas mail

8. ごく
中 □ 人
a Chinese

8. そら
□
sky

9. こう　くう
□ □ 便
airmail

10. じょう
正 □ な
normal

11. た
その □
the others

12. さま
スミス □
Mr. Smith

5 SUPPLEMENT

Another type of post box has different mailing instructions: one for letters and cards, and one for larger parcels, special delivery or international mail.

Seasonal Greeting Cards

ねんがじょう
年賀状
A New Year's Card

あけましておめでとうございます

昨年中は大変お世話になりました。

本年もよろしくお願い申し上げます。

平成六年　元旦

しょちゅうみまい
暑中見舞い
A Mid-summer Greeting

暑中見舞い申し上げます

まい日　あつい日が　つづいていますが

お元気ですか。

一九九四年　夏

どの道を通ったらいいでしょうか

As IN other countries, there are a variety of road signs in Japan, and most are written in kanji. The sign 立入禁止 tells you to keep out of the designated place. The sign 工事中 warns you to walk carefully, and 横断禁止 means no crossing a street. When walking around, it is not only helpful but fun to know the meaning of the kanji on the signs all around you. In Lessons 13 and 14, you will learn kanji that appear on different kinds of signs.

1 INTRODUCTORY QUIZ

Look at the map below and refer to the words in VOCABULARY. Then try the following quiz.

The arrows show the road Mr. Lee usually walks to Japanese language class. Because some construction work has just started, he is unable to take his usual route. While looking at the map, answer the following questions.

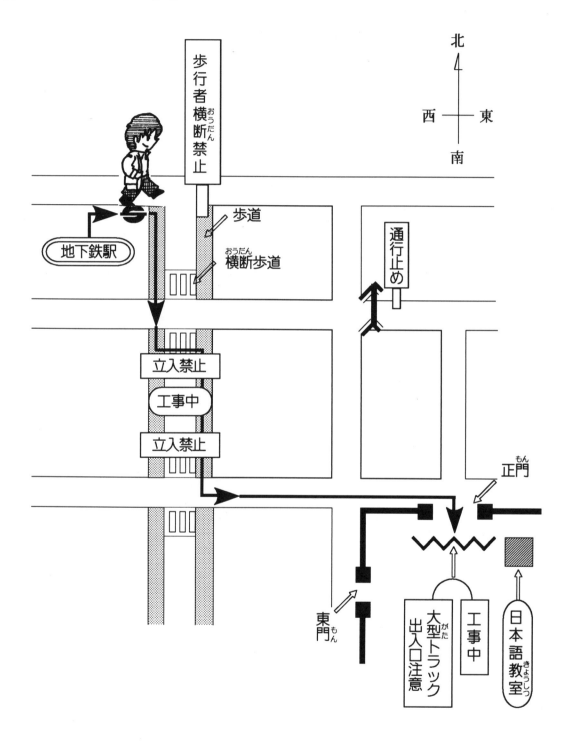

I. Choose the correct answers.

1. リーさんが地下鉄を出て、歩道をみぎへ歩いて行くと、きょうから（a. こうじ b. かじ c. ようじ）が始まって、立入禁止になっていました。

2. ですから、（a. 取る b. 通る c. 立つ）ことができません。

3. それで、横断歩道を* わたって、まっすぐ歩いて行くと、こんどは通行止めでした。そこは（a. 通れます。 b. 通れません。 c. 止まれません。）（*to cross）

4. そこでみぎにまがって歩きました。つぎに、ひだりにまがると、大学の正門も（a. 通行中 b. 歩行中 c. 工事中）で、入れませんでした。

5. 正門の前では、大型トラックがこないかどうか、よく（a. 禁止 b. 注意 c. 立入）してください。

6. リーさんは、どうして地下鉄の駅を出て、すぐ道をわたらなかったのですか。

    a. そこへ自動車がきたからです。

    b. だれも歩いていなかったからです。

    c. そこで道をわたってはいけないからです。

7. 歩道というのは、どんな道ですか。

    a. 人が歩いてはいけない道です。

    b. 歩行者のための道です。

    c. 自動車が通る道です。

II. リーさんは、きょう東門から入って日本語教室へ行きました。駅からどの道を通ったのでしょうか。ちずに書いてください。

2 VOCABULARY

Study the readings and meanings of these words to help you understand the INTRODUC-TORY QUIZ.

1.	道	みち	street, way
2.	歩道	ほ どう	sidewalk
3.	歩く	ある く	to walk
4.	工事	こう じ	construction work
5.	火事	か じ	fire
6.	用事	よう じ	business, errand
7.	立入禁止	たち いり きん し	Keep Out
8.	工事中	こう じ ちゅう	Under Construction
9.	立つ	たつ	to stand
10.	横断歩道	おう だん ほ どう	crosswalk
11.	通行止め	つう こう ど め	Closed to Traffic
12.	正門	せい もん	main gate
13.	通行中	つう こう ちゅう	while passing
14.	歩行中	ほ こう ちゅう	while walking
15.	大型トラック	おお がた トラック	big truck
16.	禁止	きん し	Prohibited
17.	注意	ちゅう い	Caution
18.	立(ち)入(り)	たち いり	entrance
19.	歩行者	ほ こう しゃ	pedestrian
20.	横断禁止	おう だん きん し	No Crossing
21.	東門	ひがし もん	east gate
22.	日本語教室	に ほん ご きょう しつ	Japanese language classroom
23.	歩行者通路	ほ こう しゃ つう ろ	pedestrian walkway

3 NEW CHARACTERS

Seven characters are introduced in this lesson. Use the explanations to help you understand and remember the characters. Study the compound words to increase your vocabulary.

道 歩 者 禁 立 注 意

163 道	street, road, path, way みち、ドウ	丶	ソ	立	ゾ	゛	首	首	首
		首	首	道	道				

道 combines 首 head or neck and ⻌ proceed or walk, and suggests walking down a road with head held high. An associated meaning is way.

 → 首

道	みち	road, street
車道	しゃどう	roadway
国道	こくどう	national road
水道	すいどう	waterworks, tap water
・・・◇・・・		
×片道×	かたみち	one-way
道路工事×	どうろ こうじ	road works / repairs
高速道路	こうそく どうろ	superhighway, expressway
柔道	じゅうどう	judo

164 歩	walk ある・く、ホ	丨	卜	止	止	歩	歩	歩	歩

歩 derives from a pictograph of two feet stepping right and left alternately, in other words, walking.

歩く	あるく	to walk
歩道××	ほどう	sidewalk, pedestrian road
横断歩道××	おうだん ほどう	pedestrian crossing, crosswalk
・・・◇・・・		

165 者	person もの、シャ	一	十	土	步	耂	者	者	者

者 originally depicted various foods cooked on a stove, and thus became associated with various gathered things (cf. 51 都). The idea of things eventually changed to people, which gave the character its present meaning.

者	もの	person
歩行者	ほこうしゃ	pedestrian
学者	がくしゃ	scholar
記者	きしゃ	journalist, reporter
・・・◇・・・		
×若者×	わかもの	young person, youth
歩行者天国	ほこうしゃ てんごく	street temporarily closed to vehicles (literally "pedestrian's paradise")
前者	ぜんしゃ	the former
後者	こうしゃ	the latter

166	prohibition キン	一	十	才	木	木	村	材	林
		林	禁	禁	禁	禁			

林 depicts two trees side by side, meaning wood, and 示 represents an altar (cf. 35 祝). Thus 禁 suggests a sacred wood surrounding an altar, into which entry is prohibited. (森, meaning forest, is larger than 林).

禁止する	きんしする	to prohibit
横断禁止	おうだん きんし	No Crossing
· · · ◇ · · ·		
駐車禁止	ちゅうしゃ きんし	No Parking
～厳禁	～げんきん	～ Strictly Prohibited

167	stand た・つ、リツ、（リッ）	1	立	六	立	立			

立 represents a man standing on the ground. Imagine a *sumō* wrestler about to stand up for a bout.

立つ	たつ	to stand
立入禁止	たちいり きんし	Keep Out
国立	こくりつ	national
市立	しりつ	municipal
· · · ◇ · · ·		
立入厳禁	たちいり げんきん	Keep Out
私立	しりつ	private (school, etc.)
中立	ちゅうりつ	neutrality
立食パーティ	りっしょく パーティ	buffet party

168	pour; pay attention, note そそ・ぐ、チュウ	`	`	シ	シ	゛シ	汁	汴	注

注 combines 氵 water and 主 stay still (cf. 75 住). When pouring water into something, one is careful to keep the hands still. Thus 注 means pouring liquid as well as paying attention.

注文する	ちゅうもんする	to order (a product)
· · · ◇ · · ·		
注ぐ	そそぐ	to pour
注目する	ちゅうもくする	to pay attention, to take notice
注射する	ちゅうしゃする	to inject

142

169 意	intention, will; meaning イ	'	一	六	六	立	产	产	音
		音	音	意	意	意			

音 by itself is sound, but as part of a kanji means being confined (cf. 138 暗). 心 means mind (cf. 125 急). The combination 意 thus indicates what is confined or kept in one's mind, such as thought, intention, or will.	注意する	ちゅういする	to be careful / cautious; to advise; to warn
	用意する	よういする	to prepare
	··· ◇ ···		
	意味	いみ	meaning, significance
	意外な	いがいな	unexpected
	頭上注意	ずじょう ちゅうい	Watch Your Head
	足元注意	あしもと ちゅうい	Watch Your Step

4 PRACTICE

Ⅰ. Write the readings of the following kanji in hiragana.

1. 歩 道　　2. 工 事　　　　3. 立 入 禁 止　　4. 通 行 止 め

5. 注 意　　6. 歩 行 者　　　7. 行 止 まり　　　8. 水 道

9. 記 者　　10. 国 立

11. この道は、工事中で通れません。

12. 車道は、人が歩くところではありません。

13. バスの中でずっと立っていたので、つかれました。

14. 本を注文しました。

Ⅱ. Fill in the blanks with appropriate kanji.

1. みち

road

2. どう

国 □

national road

3. ほ　どう

横断 □□

おう だん

crosswalk

4. ある

□ く

to walk

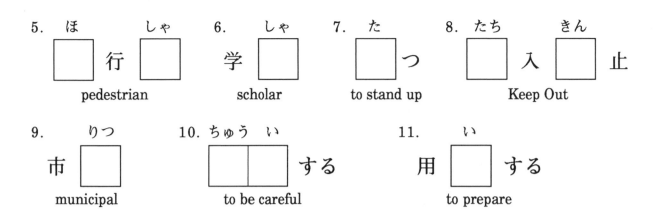

5. ほ　□ 行 □ しゃ
pedestrian

6. 学 □ しゃ
scholar

7. た □ つ
to stand up

8. たち □ 入 □ きん 止
Keep Out

9. 市 □ りつ
municipal

10. □ □ する ちゅう い
to be careful

11. 用 □ する い
to prepare

Ⅲ. Match the signs with the meanings below and write the correct letters in the parentheses.

1. ここでいちどとまって、注意しなさい。　　　　　　　　　　　　（　　）
2. 工事中ですから、ほかのみちを通ってください。　　　　　　　　（　　）
3. このさきは通れません。　　　　　　　　　　　　　　　　　　　（　　）
4. ここでは、一日中たばこをすってはいけません。　　　　　　　　（　　）
5. 火事やじしんなどの時、ここから出てください。　　　　　　　　（　　）
6. 火を消す時に使います。　　　　　　　　　　　　　　　　　　　（　　）

こたえ：　1-f　2-b　3-d　4-e　5-a　6-c

たばこは、どこですったらいいですか

IN PARKS, on the street, and at other public places, there are many signs that call your attention and issue warnings. Upon entering hotels, movie theaters, convention halls, buses, or trains, you should locate the 非常口. A 非常電話 is installed in many elevators and highway emergency parking areas. The sign 禁煙 is seen everywhere: in stations, restaurants, theaters, hospitals, and many other public places. You are encouraged to know the meanings of these signs and pay attention to them.

1 INTRODUCTORY QUIZ

Look at the illustration below and refer to the words in VOCABULARY. Then try the following quiz.

Smoking is not permitted in some public places. While visiting a park Mr. Lee wants to smoke, but he must be careful to avoid nonsmoking areas. After reading the signs below, try to advise Mr. Lee.

Choose the correct answers.

1. リーさんが、大きい木の下のベンチで、たばこをすっていた時、「そこで、たばこをすわないでください。（ a. あぶない　　b. ひじょうに　　c. しょうか ）ですから。」と、そばにいる人が注意しました。

2. 「火気厳禁」のサインの前で、リーさんは道にたばこをすてました。＊ かみくずに火がついて、火事になりそうです。リーさんは、どうすればいいですか。　（*waste paper）

    a. 右と左を確認する。

    b. 非常電話で電話する。

    c. 非常口に行く。

3. リーさんが、＊きっさ店で、たばこをすっていると、店の人が「 a. どうぞ、すってください。　b. たばこはすわないでください 」と、いいました。　　（*coffee shop）

4. それでは、リーさんは、どこでたばこをすったらいいでしょうか。

    a. 大きい木の下のベンチで

    b. きっさ店のそばのベンチで

    c. きっさ店の中で

5. リーさんが歩いて行くと、「左右確認」というサインがありました。それは、どんな＊意味ですか。　　　　　　　　　　　　　　　　　　（*meaning）

    a. 右と左、どちらへ行ってもいい

    b. 右にも左にも行ってはいけない

    c. 右と左をよくみてから行く

2　VOCABULARY

Study the readings and meanings of these words to help you understand the INTRODUC-TORY QUIZ.

1. 危険	き けん	Danger
2. 非常に	ひ じょう に	very, unusually
3. 消火	しょう か	fire extinguishing
4. 消火器	しょう か き	fire extinguisher
5. 火気厳禁	か き げん きん	Caution: Flammables
6. 右	みぎ	right
7. 左	ひだり	left
8. 非常電話	ひ じょう でん わ	emergency telephone

9. 非常口   ひ じょう ぐち   emergency exit
10. 禁煙   きん えん   No Smoking
11. 左右確認   さ ゆう かく にん   Look Left and Right

3 NEW CHARACTERS

Eight characters are introduced in this lesson. Use the explanations to help you understand and remember the characters. Study the compound words to increase your vocabulary.

気 危 険 非 消 煙 左 右

170 気	gas; spirit, mood	ノ	ｒ	ｌ	气	気	気		
	キ								

気 derives from 氣, which combines 气 breath coming out of a mouth and 米 rice (cf. 160 料). Thus 氣, or 気, indicates steam rising up from cooking rice, suggesting gas. An associated meaning is mood, which is as intangible as gas.

火気厳禁   かき げんきん   Caution: Flammables
電気   でんき   electricity
人気   にんき   popularity
· · · ◇ · · ·
空気   くうき   air
天気   てんき   weather
気体   きたい   gaseous body, gas
気分   きぶん   mood
気持(ち)   きもち   feeling

171 危	dangerous	ノ	ｒ	广	产	危	危		
	あぶ・ない、キ								

产 represents a man kneeling on the top of a cliff, and 㔾 another man at the bottom. This is dangerous, since the former may fall, and the latter may be squashed.

危ない   あぶない   dangerous, risky
· · · ◇ · · ·
危険な   きけんな   dangerous, risky

172 険　steep; harsh　ケン

フ	３	ß	ßˋ	ßへ	ßˆ	ßˇ	険
ßˆ	ßˆ	険					

険 derives from 險, which combines ß piled-up stones (cf.156 際), ∧ cover or collect, ᴗᴗ many mouths, and 从 many people. The combination 險 or 険 suggests collecting many things and piling them up until they form a harsh, steep mountain.

危険な	きけんな	dangerous, risky
	・・・◇・・・	
高電圧危険	こうでんあつ きけん	Danger: High Voltage

173 非　non-, un- (prefix)　ヒ

ノ	ョ	ヲ	ヲ	ヺ	非	非	非

非 represents the two wings of a bird stretching out in opposite directions. Not the same and not so are associated meanings. 非 is often used like the prefixes non- and un-.

非常に	ひじょうに	very, unusually, greatly
非常口	ひじょうぐち	emergency exit
非常電話	ひじょう でんわ	emergency telephone
非常ベル	ひじょう ベル	emergency bell / buzzer
	・・・◇・・・	
非売品	ひばいひん	article not for sale

174 消　put out, extinguish　け・す、ショウ

丶	丷	シ	シ丨	シˋ	シˇ	シˇ	消
消	消						

肖 was originally written 㐭, which indicated cutting meat 月 (cf. 226 肉) into smaller 小 pieces. Combined with 氵 water, 消 suggests a stream of water getting smaller and finally disappearing.

消す	けす	to put out, to extinguish; to switch off; to erase
消しゴム	けしゴム	pencil eraser
取(り)消(し)	とりけし	cancellation
消火器	しょうかき	fire extinguisher
	・・・◇・・・	
消費する	しょうひする	to consume
消防車	しょうぼうしゃ	fire engine

175 煙 smoke けむり、エン	ヽ	ン	ソ	火	火⁻	灯	炉	炉
	炳	烟	煙	煙	煙			

In ancient times, people lit 火 fires in the evening when the sun was just above the 土 ground or horizon in the 西 west. Fire is associated with 煙 smoke.

煙	けむり	smoke
禁煙する	きんえんする	to quit smoking
終日禁煙	しゅうじつ きんえん	No Smoking Any Time
· · · ◇ · · ·		
禁煙車	きんえんしゃ	nonsmoking car / table
禁煙席	きんえんせき	nonsmoking seat / table
喫煙席	きつえんせき	smoking seat
喫煙室	きつえんしつ	smoking room

---

176 左 left ひだり、サ	一	ナ	ナ	左	左			

左 combines ナ hand (cf. 88 手) and 工 carpenter's ruler (cf. 43). A carpenter usually holds a ruler with his left hand so that he can draw with his right. Thus 左 means left.

左	ひだり	left
左手	ひだりて	left hand
· · · ◇ · · ·		
左側	ひだりがわ	the left side
左折禁止	させつ きんし	No Left Turn

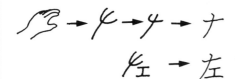

---

177 右 right みぎ、ユウ、ウ	ノ	ナ	ナ	右	右			

右 combines ナ hand and 口 mouth (cf. 107), indicating eating with one's hand. Since most people eat with their right hands, 右 has come to mean right.

右	みぎ	right
右手	みぎて	right hand
左右確認	さゆう かくにん	Look Left and Right
· · · ◇ · · ·		
右側	みぎがわ	the right side
右折禁止	うせつ きんし	No Right Turn

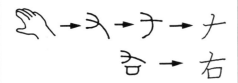

4 PRACTICE

I. Write the readings of the following kanji in hiragana.

1. 危 険　　2. 非 常 電 話　　3. 消 火　　4. 火 気 厳 禁
   (げん)

5. 禁 煙　　6. 左 右 確 認　　7. 電 気　　8. 非 常 に

9. 取 消 し　10. 煙

11. 危ないですから、気をつけてください。

12. 火事の時は、非常口から出てください。

13. 消火器で、火を消します。
    (き)

14. 地下鉄の駅は、終日禁煙です。

15. 左と右をよくみてから、わたってください。

II. Fill in the blanks with appropriate kanji.

1. ひ　　あぶ
□ 常に □ ない
very dangerous

2. ひ
□ 常ベル
emergency bell

3. き　けん
□□ な
dangerous

4. け
□ しゴム
pencil eraser

5. しょう
□ 火器
(き)
fire extinguisher

6. き　　げん
火 □ 厳 禁
Caution: Flammables

7. き
人 □
popularity

8. けむり
□
smoke

9. えん
禁 □ する
to quit smoking

10. ひだり
□ 手
left hand

11. みぎ
□ 手
right hand

12. さ　ゆう
□□
left and right

REVIEW EXERCISE Lessons 11–14

I. Fill in the blanks with appropriate kanji or their corresponding letters from the list below.

1.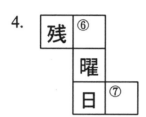

2.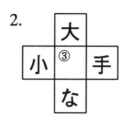

3.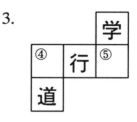

4.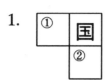

5.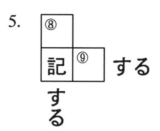

6.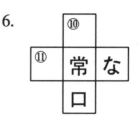

a. 切	b. 正	c. 外	d. 金	e. 者	f. 入
g. 歩	h. 航	i. 非	j. 暗	k. 際	

II. Read the following sentences and circle the correct answers.

1. （a. 郵便局，b. 電話局）へ行って、国のかぞくに速達を出しました。

2. ピーターさんは、いま（a. 外出中，b. 行き止まり）で、いません。

3. （a. 取り引き，b. 引き出し）のボタンを押します。それから、出てきたお金を取ります。

4. （a. 火気，b. 人気）のある所で、*ガソリンを扱ってはいけません。　(*gasoline)

5. 手をあげたら、タクシーが（a. 立，b. 止）まりました。

6. すみませんが、しごとの間だけ、子どもを（a. 預かって，b. 認めて）くれませんか。

キャンパス・マップ

INCLUDING JUNIOR colleges, there are approximately 1,000 universities in Japan. While mostly concentrated in large cities, some universities have recently moved their campuses into more rural areas, and a few major universities have decentralized their campuses by locating various departments in different areas. Most campus facilities include libraries, co-op stores, gymnasiums, swimming pools, and cafeterias, and some have university hospitals attached to their medical schools. Housing for faculty, staff, and students, however, tends to be very limited.

1 INTRODUCTORY QUIZ

Look at the illustration below and refer to the words in VOCABULARY. Then try the following quiz.

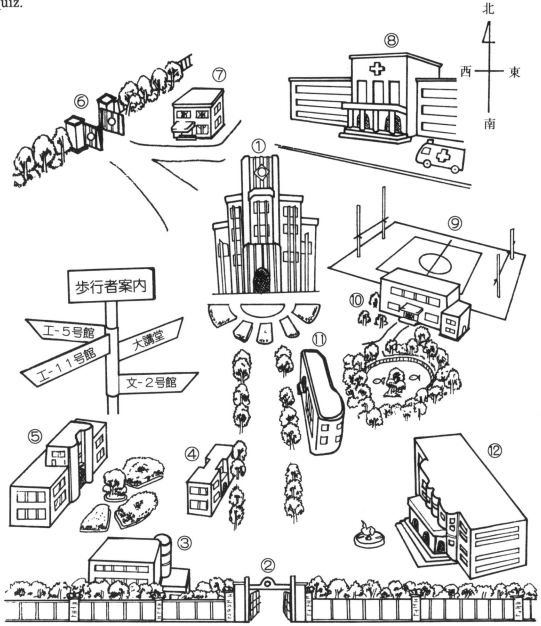

①	大講堂（中央食堂）	②	正門	③	工学部１１号館（日本語教室）
④	本部（国際交流室）	⑤	工学部１号館（リーさんの研究室）	⑥	西門
⑦	留学生センター	⑧	大学病院	⑨	グラウンド	⑩	学生会館
⑪	文学部２号館（生協）	⑫	図書館				

The parentheses indicate places that are inside buildings.

Shown opposite is a campus map of Mr. Lee's university. The sign below shows the main gate's opening and closing times. While looking at the campus map and the picture below, choose the correct answers for the following questions.

1. これは大学の地図です。リーさんは、まい日 （ a. せいもん　　b. なかもん ）から入ります。まず、自分のけんきゅうしつのある （ a. 1ごうかん　　b. 11ごうかん ）へ行きます。それから、（ a. 1号館　　b. 11号館 ）へ行って、日本語をべんきょうします。

2. ひるごはんは、大講堂の地下にある （ a. ちゅうおうしょくどう　　b. せいきょう）でたべます。午後は、本部の （ a. 西　　b. 東 ）にあるとしょかんへ行って、本やざっしをよみます。

3. グラウンドの南には （ a. 大学病院　　b. 学生会館 ）があって、ここでは、よく留学生のパーティーがあります。

4. 西門のそばにある （ a. 国際交流室　　b. 留学生センター ）でも、 いろいろな国の留学生が日本語をべんきょうしています。

5. 本やノートをかうときは、 （ a. 生協　　b. 食堂 ）へ行きます。

6. びょうきになった時は、 （ a. 大学病院　　b. 大講堂 ）へ行きます。それは、グラウンドの （ a. 北　　b. 南 ）にある大きなたてものです。

7. 正門は、 （ a. 7時　　b. 10時 ）にしまりますから、それまでに大学を出ます。

2 VOCABULARY

Study the readings and meanings of these words to help you understand the INTRODUC-TORY QUIZ.

1. 地図　　　　　　　ちず　　　　　　　　　　　　map
2. 正門　　　　　　　せい もん　　　　　　　　　main gate
3. 中門　　　　　　　なか もん　　　　　　　　　middle gate
4. 西門　　　　　　　にし もん　　　　　　　　　west gate
5. ～号館　　　　　　～ ごう かん　　　　　　　Building no. ~
6. 研究室　　　　　　けん きゅう しつ　　　　　research laboratory
7. 日本語教室　　　　に ほん ご きょう しつ　　Japanese language classroom
8. 大講堂　　　　　　だい こう どう　　　　　　large auditorium
9. 地下　　　　　　　ち か　　　　　　　　　　underground
10. 中央食堂　　　　ちゅう おう しょく どう　main cafeteria
11. 生協　　　　　　せい きょう　　　　　　　co-op
12. 本部　　　　　　ほん ぶ　　　　　　　　　headquarters
13. 図書館　　　　　と しょ かん　　　　　　library
14. グラウンド　　　　　　　　　　　　　　athletic field
15. 大学病院　　　　だい がく びょう いん　university hospital
16. 学生会館　　　　がく せい かい かん　　student hall
17. 国際交流室　　　こく さい こう りゅう しつ　International Exchange Office
18. 留学生センター　りゅう がく せい センター　Foreign Students' Center
19. 開門　　　　　　かい もん　　　　　　　　gate opening
20. 閉門　　　　　　へい もん　　　　　　　　gate closing

3 NEW CHARACTERS

Nine characters are introduced in this lesson. Use the explanations to help you understand and remember the characters. Study the compound words to increase your vocabulary.

講 堂 食 門 館 会 協 図 閉

178 講

lecture, study

コウ

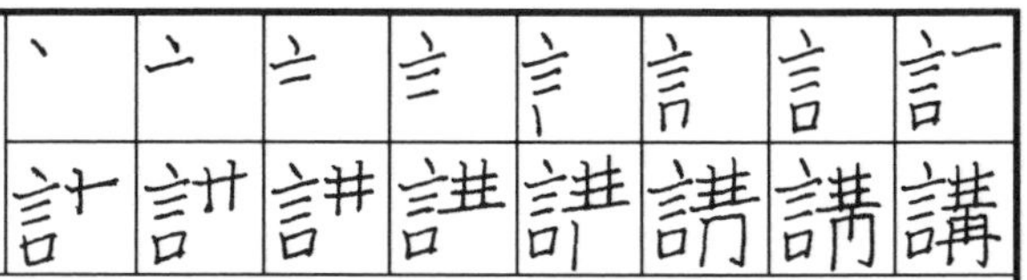

講 combines 言 speak and 冓, which represents two identical wooden frames and indicates shared common elements. Thus 講 means lecture, during which someone speaks to listeners about a subject of common interest.

開講する	かいこうする	to open / begin a course
休講	きゅうこう	no lecture
	···◇···	
講師	こうし	lecturer
講演する	こうえんする	to give a lecture, to deliver an address
講座	こうざ	lecture course; professorial chair
講習会	こうしゅうかい	short training course

179 堂

big building, hall

ドウ

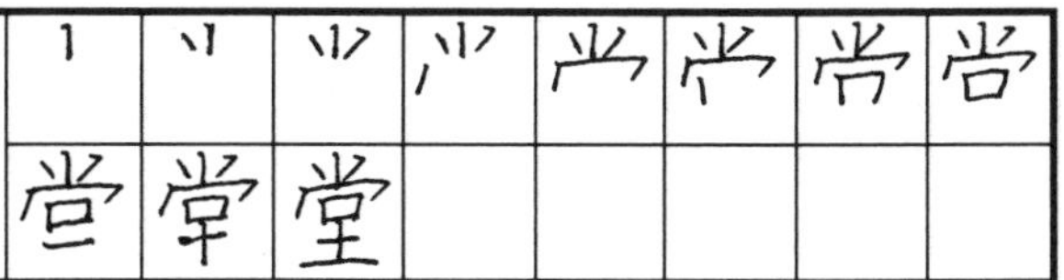

堂 combines 尚 smoke rising up high above a stove (cf. 159 常) and 土 ground. Thus 堂 means tall building on the ground.

講堂	こうどう	auditorium
	···◇···	
公会堂	こうかいどう	public / town hall
国会議事堂	こっかい ぎじどう	the Diet Building

180 食

eat, meal

た・べる、ショク、(ショッ)

食 depicts a bowl of cooked rice (cf. 11 百) resting on a stand with a lid on top, and suggests meal and eating.

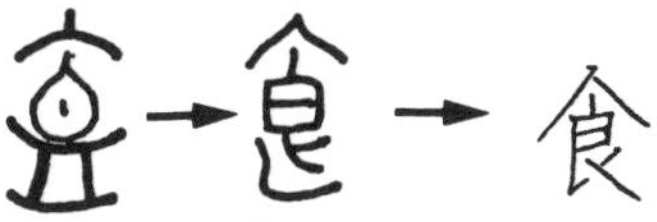

食べる	たべる	to eat
食堂	しょくどう	dining room, cafeteria
食事する	しょくじする	to have a meal
定食	ていしょく	set meal
食券	しょっけん	meal ticket / coupon
	···◇···	
外食する	がいしょくする	to eat out, to eat at a restaurant
食前	しょくぜん	before meals
食後	しょくご	after meals
食間	しょっかん	between meals

181 門 gate モン		一	冂	冂	冂	冂	門	門	門

門 derives from a pictograph of a gate.

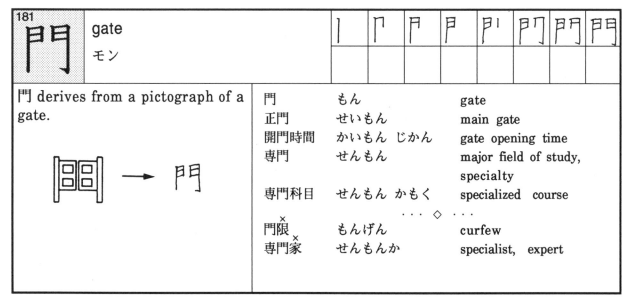

門	もん	gate
正門	せいもん	main gate
開門時間	かいもん じかん	gate opening time
専門	せんもん	major field of study, specialty
専門科目	せんもん かもく	specialized course
	・・・ ◇ ・・・	
門限	もんげん	curfew
専門家	せんもんか	specialist, expert

182 館 building, hall カン		ノ	入	入	今	今	今	食	食
		食`	食`	食宀	飠宀	飠宀	飠宀	館	館

館 combines 飠 (a variation of 食) eat, and 官, a rich bureaucrat with a puffed-up stomach in a house. 館 formerly meant a building where bureaucrats ate, and now has come to mean public building or hall.

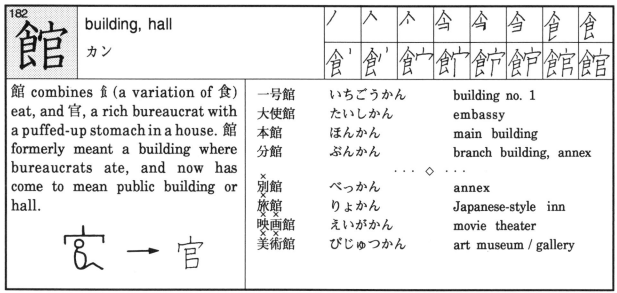

一号館	いちごうかん	building no. 1
大使館	たいしかん	embassy
本館	ほんかん	main building
分館	ぶんかん	branch building, annex
	・・・ ◇ ・・・	
別館	べっかん	annex
旅館	りょかん	Japanese-style inn
映画館	えいがかん	movie theater
美術館	びじゅつかん	art museum / gallery

183 会 meet, meeting, association あ・う、カイ		ノ	入	厽	亼	会	会		

会 combines 亼 collect or gather, and 云 being surrounded on all four sides. From these concepts, 会 has come to mean meet, meeting, or association.

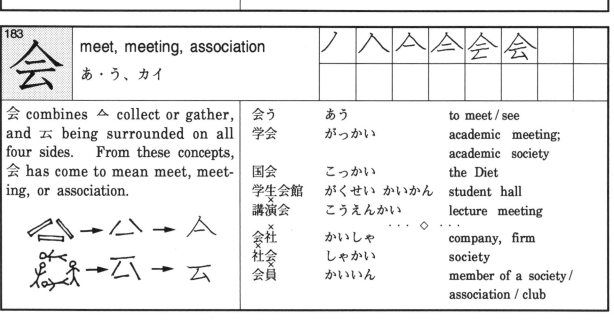

会う	あう	to meet / see
学会	がっかい	academic meeting; academic society
国会	こっかい	the Diet
学生会館	がくせい かいかん	student hall
講演会	こうえんかい	lecture meeting
	・・・ ◇ ・・・	
会社	かいしゃ	company, firm
社会	しゃかい	society
会員	かいいん	member of a society / association / club

184 協	cooperation キョウ	一	十	十フ	十カ	忄カ	协	協	協

十 ten suggests adding five and five, and 力 indicates power or force (cf. 67 男). Thus 協 can be thought of as combining three forces together in an act of cooperation.

生協	せいきょう	co-op
協会	きょうかい	society, association
アジア学生協会	アジア がくせい きょうかい	Asian Students' Association
· · · ◇ · · ·		
協力する	きょうりょくする	to cooperate
国際協力	こくさい きょうりょく	international cooperation

---

185 図	drawing, diagram ズ、ト	`	冂	𠃌	门	汉	図	図	

図 derives from 圖, which combines 啚 a grain storehouse and farm land, and 囗 paper. 圖, or 図, originally indicated a map drawn on a sheet of paper, and came to mean drawing or diagram in general.

図	ず	figure, diagram
図-3	ず-さん	Figure 3
地図	ちず	map
案内図	あんないず	guide / information map
図書館	としょかん	library
· · · ◇ · · ·		
図表	ずひょう	charts, figures, and tables
図面	ずめん	drawing

---

186 閉	close, shut し・まる、し・める、ヘイ		ノ	冂	尸	戶	戸	門	門	門
		門	閉	閉						

閉 represents a gate with a cross bar that closes to prevent people from entering.

閉まる	しまる	to close (vi.)
閉める	しめる	to close (vt.)
閉会する	へいかいする	to close a meeting; for a meeting to close
閉門時間	へいもん じかん	gate closing time
· · · ◇ · · ·		
閉館する	へいかんする	to close (a library, hall, etc.)
開閉	かいへい	opening and shutting
閉会式	へいかいしき	closing ceremony

4 PRACTICE

Ⅰ. Write the readings of the following kanji in hiragana.

1. 地 図   2. 西 門   3. 〜 号 館   4. 大 講 堂

5. 中 央 食 堂 6. 生 協   7. 図 書 館   8. 学 生 会 館

9. 閉 門   10. 休 講   11. 食 事   12. 食 券

13. 専 門   14. 本 館   15. 国 会   16. 協 会

17. 案 内 図   18. 閉 会 する

19. まい日、生協の食堂で、ひるごはんを食べます。

20. よるは、門をかならず閉めてください。

21. 正門は、午後十時に閉まります。

22. ではあした、大使館で会いましょう。

Ⅱ. Fill in the blanks with appropriate kanji.

1.　こう　どう
大 ☐ ☐
large auditorium

2.　た
☐ べる
to eat

3.　しょく
定 ☐
set meal

4.　もん
専 ☐ 科目
specialized course

5.　かん
分 ☐
branch building

6.　あ
☐ う
to meet

7.　きょう かい
アジア学生 ☐ ☐
Asian Students' Association

8.　ず
地 ☐
map

9.　と　　かん
☐ 書 ☐
library

10.　へい もん
☐ ☐ 時間
gate closing time

大学のたてものの中

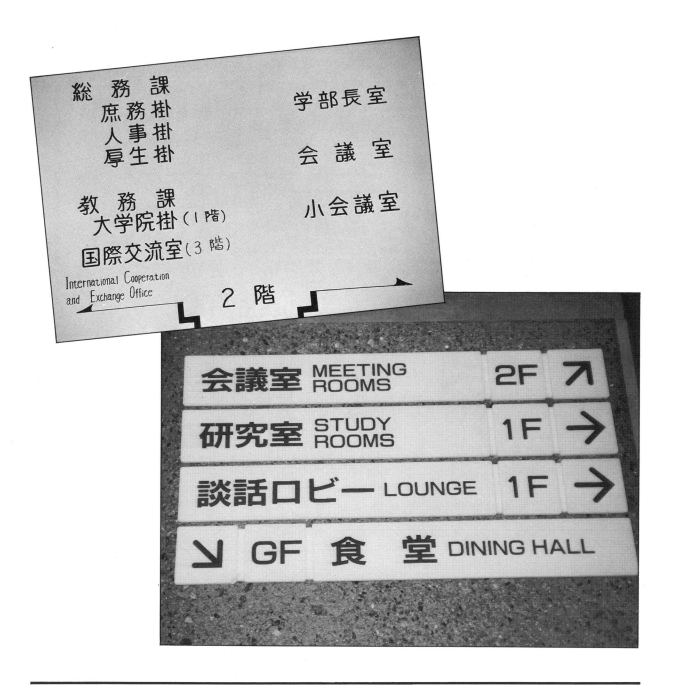

As CAN be expected, many kinds of rooms are found in university buildings; for example, lecture rooms, conference rooms, study rooms, and offices. The names of the rooms are often written on signs in kanji. This lesson will help you recognize kanji for these rooms.

1 INTRODUCTORY QUIZ

Look at the illustration below and refer to the words in VOCABULARY. Then try the following quiz.

I. Here is the first floor layout of a university building where Mr. Lee studies. While looking at the floor plan, choose the correct answers to the questions below.

一階

入口

一階の案内

① 小会議室　② 講義室　③ 図書室　④ 研究室
⑤ 大会議室　⑥ 教授室　⑦ 女子手洗い　⑧ 男子手洗い
⑨ 事務室　⑩ コピー室　⑪ 実験室

1. 入口の左には、（ a. じむ室　b. じっけん室 ）があります。

2. しょうかいぎ室のとなりは、（ a. としょ室　b. こうぎ室 ）です。

3. 一階には、（ a. けんきゅう室　b. しょくどう ）はありません。

4. 学生は、（ a. 大会議室　b. 研究室 ）でべんきょうします。

5. 専門のクラスは、（ a. 講義室　b. 事務室 ）であります。

6. 本やざっしがよみたい時は、（ a. 実験室　b. 図書室 ）へ行けばいいです。

II. The names of the rooms are usually posted over the doors. The signs hanging on the doors show whether each room is vacant or occupied. Look at the picture below and choose the correct answers to the following questions.

1. 講義室と研究室の間に、（ a. としょ室　　b. しょうかいぎ室 ）があります。

2. 小会議室は、いま（ a. 使えます。　　b. 使えません。 ）

3. 講義室は、いま（ a. あいています。　　b. 使っています。 ）

III. Combine these kanji to make compounds, and then write the kanji in the spaces below.

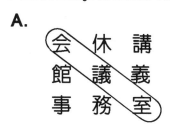

A.

会	休	講
館	議	義
事	務	室

B.

一	番	研
階	号	究
実	験	室

A. 1. Ex. 会議室　　　　　　

2. _____

3. _____

4. _____

5. _____

B. 1. _____

2. _____

3. _____

4. _____

5. _____

2 VOCABULARY

Study the readings and meanings of these words to help you understand the INTRODUCTORY QUIZ.

1. 一階 　　　　　いっ かい 　　　　　the 1st floor
2. 研究室 　　　　けん きゅう しつ 　　research laboratory, research unit
3. 事務室 　　　　じ む しつ 　　　　　administrative office
4. 実験室 　　　　じっ けん しつ 　　　laboratory for experiments
5. 会議室 　　　　かい ぎ しつ 　　　　conference room
6. 図書室 　　　　と しょ しつ 　　　　library room
7. 講義室 　　　　こう ぎ しつ 　　　　lecture room
8. 教授室 　　　　きょう じゅ しつ 　　professor's office
9. 空室 　　　　　くう しつ 　　　　　Vacant Room
10. 使用中 　　　　し よう ちゅう 　　　Occupied
11. コピー室 　　　コピー しつ 　　　　photocopy room

3 NEW CHARACTERS

Nine characters are introduced in this lesson. Use the explanations to help you understand and remember the characters. Study the compound words to increase your vocabulary.

階 義 議 室 研 究 務 実 験

187 階	stair, story; rank カイ、（ガイ）	フ	3	阝	阝-	阝ヒ	阝ヒ′	阝ヒヒ	阝ヒヒ
		阝ヒヒ	阝ヒヒ	阝ヒヒ	階				

階 combines 阝 stone hedge, 比 two men lined up, and 白 modified from 自 oneself (cf. 99). In ancient times, people piled up stones to make stairs. Rank is an associated meaning. By itself 皆 means everybody.

四階	よんかい	the fourth floor
地下一階	ちか いっかい	the first basement
三階	さんがい	the third floor
・・・◇・・・		
階段	かいだん	staircase, stairs
地階	ちかい	basement

164

188	justice, righteousness	、	`	立	业	羊	羊	羊
義 ギ		羊	莠	義	義	義		

義 combines 羊 beautiful or right (cf. 131 着), and 我, a hand holding a weapon to protect oneself, meaning I. Thus 義 means a right way of doing something, which is related to the idea of justice.

講義する	こうぎする	to give a lecture
· · · ◇ · · ·		
主義	しゅぎ	principle, -ism
定義する	ていぎする	to define
意義	いぎ	meaning, significance
正義	せいぎ	justice
義理	ぎり	social duty, obligation; in-law

189	deliberate, discuss	、	亠	言	言	言	言	言	言
議 ギ		詳	詳	詳	謙	謙	議	議	議

議 which combines 言 speak and 義 justice or righteousness, means discussing and deliberating to come to right conclusions.

会議	かいぎ	meeting, conference
国際会議	こくさい かいぎ	international conference
· · · ◇ · · ·		
議論する	ぎろんする	to argue, to discuss
議題	ぎだい	subject for discussion, agenda
議長	ぎちょう	chairperson
議会	ぎかい	assembly, the Diet, Congress, Parliament
議員	ぎいん	member of an assembly / the Diet / Congress / Parliament

---

190	room	'	'	宀	宀	宧	宧	宰	室
室 シツ		室							

室 combines 宀 house and 至 bird diving down to the ground, meaning reaching a goal. Thus 室 means room, which can be thought of as the goal to reach in a house.

会議室	かいぎしつ	conference room
図書室	としょしつ	library room
講義室	こうぎしつ	lecture room
空室	くうしつ	vacant room
地下室	ちかしつ	basement
· · · ◇ · · ·		
五号室	ごごうしつ	room no. 5
室内	しつない	indoor, inside the room
浴室	よくしつ	bathroom

191 研 — polish, sharpen / ケン

一 ノ 了 石 石 石 石 研 研

研, which combines 石 stone (cf. 140 確) and 开 make things even, indicates making something smooth with a stone, namely, polishing or sharpening.

羊羊 → 开 → 开

~研	~けん	abbreviation for ~研究所/室 (~ Research Institute / Laboratory)

... ◇ ...

研修生	けんしゅうせい	trainee

192 究 — investigate / キュウ

' ' 宀 宀 穴 空 究

究 combines 穴 hole (cf. 158 空), and 九 nine, the number that ends the series of single digits. Thus 究 means searching or investigating an unknown space to its end.

研究する	けんきゅうする	to research, to investigate
研究室	けんきゅうしつ	research laboratory; research unit
研究生	けんきゅうせい	research student
研究所	けんきゅうじょ	research institute
研究会	けんきゅうかい	research society / meeting

... ◇ ...

研究員	けんきゅういん	research fellow

193 務 — work; serve / ム

フ マ ヌ 予 矛 矛 矛 矛 務 務

務 combines 矛 halberd, 力 power (cf. 67 男), and 攵, indicating an action (cf. 47 攻). Fighting powerfully with a halberd was an important duty of warriors. From this association, 務 came to mean work in general.

ψ → 予 → 矛

事務室	じむしつ	office, administrative office
事務所	じむしょ	office

... ◇ ...

義務教育	ぎむ きょういく	compulsory education
公務員	こうむいん	government employee, public servant
外務省	がいむしょう	Ministry of Foreign Affairs
法務省	ほうむしょう	Ministry of Justice
勤務先	きんむさき	one's place of work

| 194 実 | fruit; truth, actuality
み、ジツ、（ジッ） | ノ | ハ | 宀 | 宀 | 宇 | 宇 | 実 | 実 |

実 derives from 實, which combines 宀 house, 毌 or 田 rice paddy (cf. 87), and 貝 money (cf. 200 費). Thus 實 or 実 implies a fruitful harvest, which means fruit or nuts as well as actual money for a household. Truth is an associated meaning.

事実	じじつ	fact
実際	じっさい	fact, reality; actually
· · · ◇ · · ·		
木の実	きのみ	nut
実物	じつぶつ	real / actual thing
実用	じつよう	practical use
実習する	じっしゅうする	to have practical training
実行する	じっこうする	to execute, to implement

| 195 験 | test, examine
ケン | 1 | 厂 | 厂 | 厍 | 厍 | 馬 | 馬 | 馬 |
| | | 馬 | 馬 | 馬 | 馬 | 馬 | 馬 | 馬 | 験 |

験 derives from 驗, which combines 馬 horse (cf. 70 駅) and 僉 collect many things (cf. 172 険). The ancient Chinese examined and tested many horses before buying one.

実験する	じっけんする	to conduct an experiment
実験室	じっけんしつ	laboratory for experiments
· · · ◇ · · ·		
試験	しけん	test, examination
経験する	けいけんする	to experience, to go through
体験する	たいけんする	to experience personally, to go through

4 PRACTICE

I. Write the readings of the following kanji in hiragana.

1. 事 務 室　2. 実 験 室　3. 講 義 室　4. 一 階　　5. 研 究 室

6. 三 階　　7. 研 究 生　8. 事 実　　9. 実 験 する

10. 食堂は、地下二階にあります。

11. 来月、京都で国際会議があります。

12. いま、大会議室は使用中ですが、小会議室は空室です。

13. それは、実際にあったことです。

II. Fill in the blanks with the appropriate kanji.

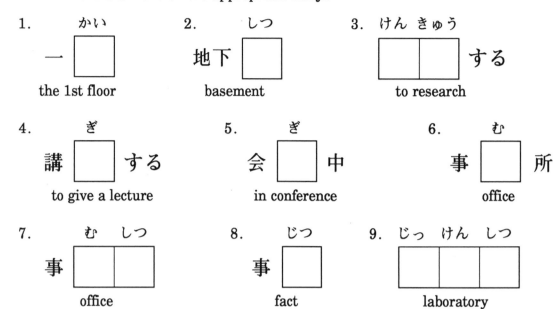

1.　かい
一☐
the 1st floor

2.　しつ
地下☐
basement

3.　けん　きゅう
☐☐する
to research

4.　ぎ
講☐する
to give a lecture

5.　ぎ
会☐中
in conference

6.　む
事☐所
office

7.　む　しつ
事☐☐
office

8.　じつ
事☐
fact

9.　じっ　けん　しつ
☐☐☐
laboratory

なんのお知らせですか

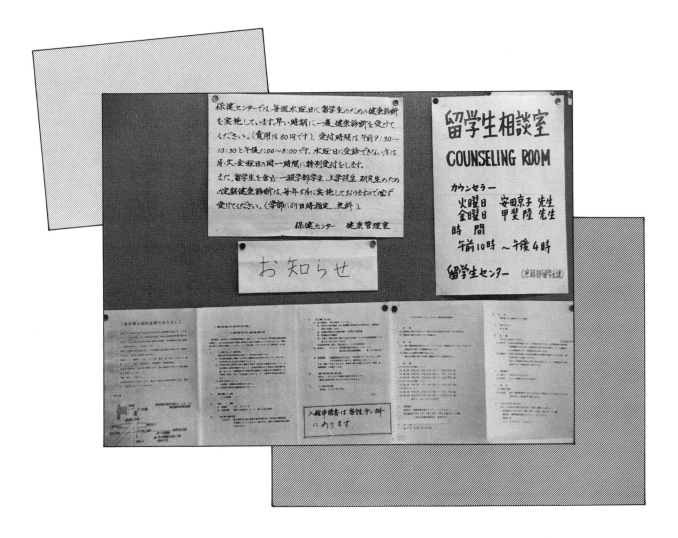

CAMPUS BULLETIN boards contain a lot of useful information, such as dates of final exams, when new courses start, names of scholarship recipients, and so on. Municipal offices, supermarkets, banks, and other public places also use bulletin boards for official notices and personal advertisements. Thanks to ads on bulletin boards, you can find part-time jobs, used CD players, or bicycles at discount prices. Sometimes if you are lucky, you can even get things such as used furniture or electrical appliances for free. The community bulletin boards give you the latest news in your neighborhood and the schedule of local events. In this lesson, you will learn how to read bulletin boards and, in the process, you may even find some useful information on boards where you work or study.

1 INTRODUCTORY QUIZ

Look at the illustration below and refer to the words in VOCABULARY. Then try the following quiz.

I. Posted below is a notice about a lecture by Professor Brown of London University. Read the notice carefully and write the correct answers in the spaces provided.

講演会のお知らせ

" 新しい都市について "

日時： ２月２４日（金）
　　　 1:30〜3:00 p.m.
会場： 工学部　１１号館
　　　 ４階　　二番教室
講師： ブラウン教授
　　　　（ロンドン大学）

1. ブラウン教授は、なにについて話しますか。
　　＿＿＿＿＿＿＿＿＿＿＿＿について話します。
2. 講演をききたいのですが、どのたてものに行けばいいですか。
　　＿＿＿＿＿＿＿＿＿＿＿＿に行けばいいです。
3. 四階のどのへやに行けばいいですか。
　　＿＿＿＿＿＿＿＿＿＿＿＿に行けばいいです。
4. ブラウン教授の講演はなん日ですか。
　　＿＿＿＿＿＿＿＿＿＿＿＿です。

Ⅱ. Below is a notice about a field trip to the Yokohama Bay Bridge. To join the trip you must fill in the application form. Read the notice and write the correct answers in the spaces provided.

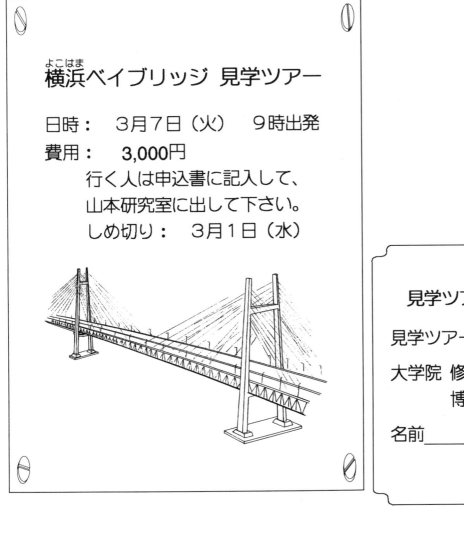

横浜ベイブリッジ　見学ツアー
（よこはま）

日時：　３月７日（火）　９時出発
費用：　3,000円
　　　　行く人は申込書に記入して、
　　　　山本研究室に出して下さい。
　　　　しめ切り：　３月１日（水）

見学ツアー申込書

見学ツアーに行きます。

大学院　修士（　　）年
　　　　博士（　　）年

名前＿＿＿＿＿＿＿＿＿＿

1. 見学ツアーはなん日ですか。
＿＿＿＿＿＿＿＿＿＿＿＿＿です。
2. お金はいくらかかりますか。
＿＿＿＿＿＿＿＿＿＿＿＿＿かかります。
3. 見学ツアーに行きたい人はどうすればいいですか。
＿＿＿＿＿＿＿＿＿＿＿に記入して、＿＿＿＿＿＿＿＿＿＿＿＿に出します。
4. いつまでに出さなければなりませんか。
＿＿＿＿＿＿＿＿＿＿＿＿＿までに出さなければなりません。
5. しゅうしコースの学生も、はかせコースの学生も行けますか。
＿＿＿＿＿＿＿＿＿＿＿＿＿＿＿＿＿＿。

Application Form for a Certificate of Student Status or Proof of Graduation

証明書交付願			
		請求年月日　平成　　年　　月　　日	
入　学 年月日	平成　年　月　日 　　　　　　入　学	修了（見込） 年　　月	平成　　年　　月　修　了 　　　　　　　修了見込
専　攻	専　攻	ローマ字	
課　程	修士　・　博士	氏　名	㊞
学生証番号		年　　　月　　　日生	
住　所	（〒　　）		
		電話　　（　　）	
使用目的			
提出先			

Course Registration Form

履修科目届		
	平成　年度　　学期	
科目担当者名		
科目番号		単位
科目名		
上記科目を申告します。		
所属	修士　・　博士	専攻
学生証番号		
氏名		

These forms are available at the administrative office.

2 VOCABULARY

Study the readings and meanings of these words to help you understand the INTRODUCTORY QUIZ.

1.	お知らせ	お し らせ	notice
2.	教授	きょう じゅ	professor
3.	講師	こう し	lecturer
4.	ロンドン大学	ロンドン だい がく	London University
5.	講演会	こう えん かい	lecture
6.	会場	かい じょう	lecture hall
7.	～番教室	～ ばん きょう しつ	classroom no. ~
8.	講演する	こう えん する	to give a lecture
9.	見学ツアー	けん がく ツアー	field trip
10.	横浜ベイブリッジ	よこ はま ベイブリッジ	Yokohama Bay Bridge
11.	費用	ひ よう	cost
12.	出発	しゅっ ぱつ	departure
13.	山本研究室	やま もと けん きゅう しつ	Yamamoto Research Laboratory
14.	しめ切り	しめ きり	deadline
15.	大学院	だい がく いん	graduate school
16.	修士	しゅう し	master degree
17.	博士	はく し	doctoral degree
18.	～証明書交付願	～ しょう めい しょ こう ふ ねがい	application for ~ certificate
19.	学生証	がく せい しょう	student ID card
20.	履修科目届	り しゅう か もく とどけ	course registration

3 NEW CHARACTERS

Eleven characters are introduced in this lesson. Use the explanations to help you understand and remember the characters. Study the compound words to increase your vocabulary.

知 場 教 見 費 院 修 士 博 明 届

196 知 — know
し・る、チ

ノ	ム	匕	矢	矢	矢口	知	知

知, which combines 矢 arrow and 口 mouth, suggests speaking straight and accurately. In order to do so, knowledge of the subject is required.

知る	しる	to know
お知らせ	おしらせ	information, notice
通知する	つうちする	to notify, to inform
知事	ちじ	prefectural governor
· · · ◇ · · ·		
知(り)合い	しりあい	acquaintance
知識	ちしき	knowledge
知人	ちじん	acquaintance

197 場 — place
ば、ジョウ

一	十	土	均	切	坦	垣	垣
坦	堤	場	場				

場 combines ±(土) ground and 昜 sun rising high and shining brightly. From indicating a place where the sun shines on the ground, 場 has come to mean place in general.

場所	ばしょ	place, location
工場	こうじょう	factory
会場	かいじょう	meeting / party / lecture / exhibition place
入場券	にゅうじょうけん	admission / platform ticket
· · · ◇ · · ·		
場合	ばあい	case, occasion
現場	げんば	the scene (of accident, etc.); work site
場内	じょうない	inside the place
駐車場	ちゅうしゃじょう	parking lot

198 教 — teach
おし・える、キョウ

一	十	土	耂	考	考	孝	孝
孝	教	教					

教 combines 耂, simplified 老, depicting an old man, 子 child (cf. 117), and 攵, indicating an action (cf. 47 攻). Together they suggest an old man teaching a child.

教える	おしえる	to teach
教室	きょうしつ	classroom
教科書	きょうかしょ	textbook
· · · ◇ · · ·		
教授	きょうじゅ	professor
教師	きょうし	teacher
教務課	きょうむか	Academic Affairs Section
宗教	しゅうきょう	religion

199 見 — see, watch — み・る、ケン

丨	冂	冂	月	目	見	見

見 combines 目 eye and 儿 legs, a reference to man. A man's eyes enable him to see.

見る	みる	to see, to watch
見本	みほん	sample
見学する	けんがくする	to visit (a factory, etc.) for study
意見	いけん	opinion

· · · ◇ · · ·

見出し	みだし	headline
発見する	はっけんする	to discover
記者会見	きしゃ かいけん	press conference

200 費 — cost, extend; spend — つい・やす、ヒ、（ピ）

一	二	弓	弔	弗	弗	弗	曹
費	費	費	費				

費 combines 弗, a vine being untangled by two sticks, meaning split, and 貝 shell, which was formerly used as money. Money being split up to cover various expenses has given 費 the meaning of spend or expense.

費用	ひよう	expense, cost
食費	しょくひ	food expenses
学費	がくひ	school expenses
会費	かいひ	membership fee
交通費	こうつうひ	transportation expenses

· · · ◇ · · ·

費やす	ついやす	to spend
国費	こくひ	national expenditure
私費	しひ	private expense
実費	じっぴ	actual expense
消費者	しょうひしゃ	consumer

201 院 — institution — イン

⁊	阝	阝	阝'	阝'	阝宀	阝宀	阝宀
阝宁	院						

院 represents a building 宀 surrounded by a stone wall 阝 where bald men 元 such as priests or scholars used to work. Thus 院 stands for temples, hospitals, and other institutions.

大学院	だいがくいん	graduate school
大学院生	だいがくいんせい	graduate student
入院する	にゅういんする	to be hospitalized

· · · ◇ · · ·

美容院	びよういん	beauty parlor
退院する	たいいんする	to be discharged from a hospital
寺院	じいん	temple

202 修 master; mend

シュウ

ノ イ 仁 仃 俨 俏 攸 修 修 修

修 combines 彡 hair ornament and 攸 pouring water on someone's back, both suggesting putting something into good shape. From this 修 has come to mean master something.

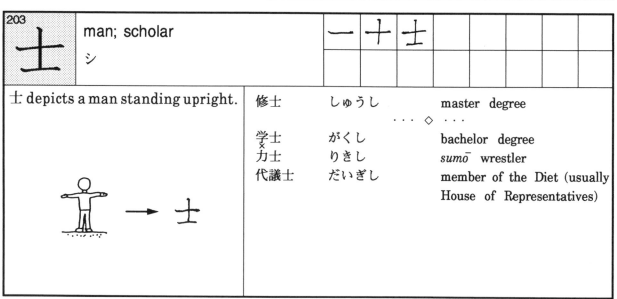

研修	けんしゅう	on-the-job training
研修生	けんしゅうせい	trainee
・・・◇・・・		
修了証書	しゅうりょう しょうしょ	certificate of completion
修学旅行	しゅうがく りょこう	school excursion
修理する	しゅうりする	to mend, to repair
修正する	しゅうせいする	to amend, to correct

203 士 man; scholar

シ

一 十 士

士 depicts a man standing upright.

修士	しゅうし	master degree
・・・◇・・・		
学士	がくし	bachelor degree
力士	りきし	*sumō* wrestler
代議士	だいぎし	member of the Diet (usually House of Representatives)

204 博 broad, extensive

ハク、(パク)

一 十 十一 忭 忭 忭 忭 忭
忭 博 博 博

博, which combines 十 add (cf. 184 協), 専 specialize (cf. 46), and 丶 point, suggests broadening one's specialization by adding various points to one's knowledge. From this 博 has come to mean broad or extensive.

博士	はくし／*はかせ	doctoral degree; doctor
工学博士	こうがく はくし／ *はかせ	Doctor of Engineering
・・・◇・・・		
博物館	はくぶつかん	museum of history and culture
万博	ばんぱく	abbreviation for 万国博覧会 (world exposition)

205 明	bright, clear; next あか・るい、メイ	丨	刀	月	日	日)	明	明	明

When the sun 日 and the moon 月 come together, everything becomes bright.

明るい	あかるい	bright
証明する	しょうめいする	to prove, to certify
証明書	しょうめいしょ	certificate
証明証	しょうめいしょう	certificate
･･･ ◇ ･･･		
×説明書	せつめいしょ	explanatory booklet, manual
文明	ぶんめい	civilization
明日	*あす／*あした	tomorrow

206 届	reach; deliver; notify とど・く、とど・ける		⼁	尸	尸	吊	届	届

届 combines 尸 reclining man and 由 bottle of wine. From the idea of delivering wine to a sick person, 届 has come to mean deliver. Reach is an associated meaning.

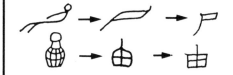

届く	とどく	(a letter, etc.) to reach / arrive
届ける	とどける	to deliver; to notify
届(け)	とどけ	notification
履修科目届	りしゅう かもく とどけ	course registration
･･･ ◇ ･･･		
受講届×	じゅこうとどけ	course registration
変更届×	へんこうとどけ	notice of change of ~
欠席届×	けっせきとどけ	absentee notice
届け先	とどけさき	delivery destination

4 PRACTICE

I. Write the readings of the following kanji in hiragana.

1. お知らせ　　2. 教授　　　　3. 会場　　　　4. 見学ツアー

5. 費用　　　　6. 大学院　　7. 修士　　　　8. 博士

9. 証明書　　10. 届ける　　11. 通知する　　12. 履修科目届

13. 教科書　　14. 工場　　　15. 食費　　　　16. 入院する

17. 講演会の場所を教えてください。

18. 工場で、研修します。

19. この教室は、明るいですね。

20. 交通費は、自分で出さなければなりません。

Ⅱ. Fill in the blanks with appropriate kanji.

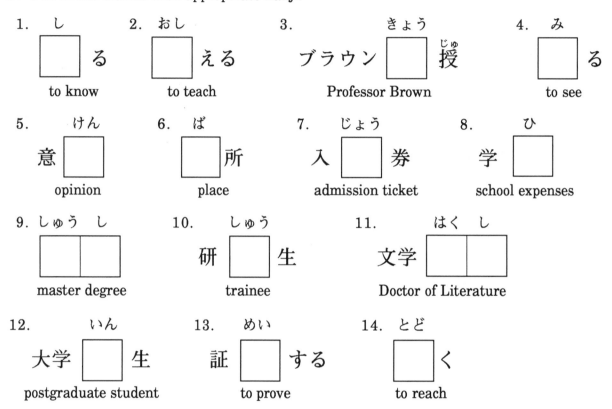

1. し
□る
to know

2. おし
□える
to teach

3. きょう
ブラウン□授
Professor Brown

4. み
□る
to see

5. けん
意□
opinion

6. ば
□所
place

7. じょう
入□券
admission ticket

8. ひ
学□
school expenses

9. しゅう し
□□
master degree

10. しゅう
研□生
trainee

11. はく し
文学□□
Doctor of Literature

12. いん
大学□生
postgraduate student

13. めい
証□する
to prove

14. とど
□く
to reach

病院へ行きます

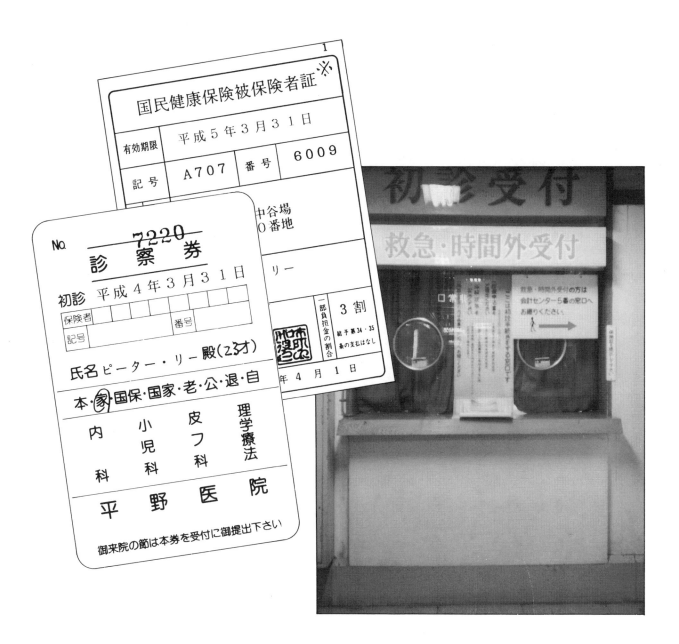

IF YOU become ill, you may decide to visit a neighborhood clinic or a large hospital. One convenient aspect of a small clinic is that you can make an appointment to see a doctor, receive medicine, and make payments all at one window. Larger hospitals are more bureaucratic and each window has a different function. In this lesson, you will study some kanji frequently seen in hospitals, as well as kanji found in instructions for taking medicine.

1 INTRODUCTORY QUIZ

Look at the illustrations below and refer to the words in VOCABULARY. Then try the following quiz.

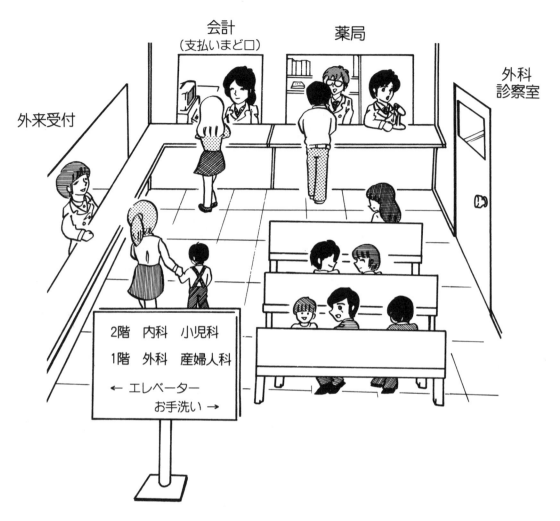

Ⅰ. Match the right and left phrases. Write the correct letters (a〜d) in the spaces provided.

1. Mr. Lee has come to the hospital. Help him out by telling him what to do at each window.

1) 外来受付 ( ) a. お医者さんにみてもらう

2) 会計（支払いまど口） ( ) b. くすりをもらう

3) 薬局 ( ) c. お金をはらう

4) 診察室 ( ) d. 保険証や診察券を出す

2. Which medical departments should he go to for the following complaints?

1) *かぜをひいた時 ( ) a. 外科 (*a cold)

2) *はがいたい時 ( ) b. 内科 (*a toothache)

3) 子どもが病気になった時 ( ) c. 歯科

4) *けがをした時 ( ) d. 小児科 (*an injury)

II. Mr. Lee has received his medicine. Refer to the instructions on the prescription envelope, and then choose the correct answers to the questions below.

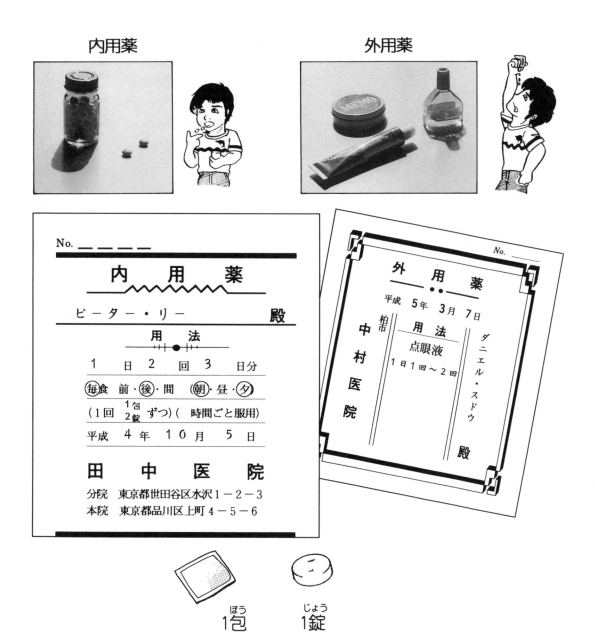

1. のむ薬はどちらですか。　　　　　　　　a. 外用薬　　b. 内用薬

2. リーさんはどのぐらい薬をもらいましたか。　（ a. 二　　b. 三　　c. 四 ）か分

3. 一日、なん回のみますか。　　　　　　　　（ a. 一　　b. 二　　c. 三 ）回

4. いつ、のみますか。
　　　　　　　　　　　　a. 朝食と夕食のあと、ときどき
　　　　　　　　　　　　b. 朝食と夕食のあと、いつも
　　　　　　　　　　　　c. 朝食か夕食のあと、どちらか

5. 毎回、いくつ、のみますか。　　　　　　　（ a. 一　　b. 二　　c. 三 ）包
　　　　　　　　　　　　　　　　　　　　　（ a. 一　　b. 二　　c. 三 ）錠

2 VOCABULARY

Study the readings and meanings of these words to help you understand the INTRODUC-
TORY QUIZ.

1. 病院	びょう いん	hospital
2. 病気	びょう き	sickness
3. 外来受付	がい らい うけ つけ	outpatient reception
4. 会計	かい けい	bill, payment
5. 支払いまど口	し はら い まど ぐち	payment window
6. 薬局	やっ きょく	pharmacy
7. 診察室	しん さつ しつ	examination room
8. 医者	い しゃ	medical doctor
9. 診察券	しん さつ けん	patient's card
10. 保険証	ほ けん しょう	health insurance certificate
11. 外科	げ か	surgery
12. 内科	ない か	internal medicine unit
13. 産婦人科	さん ふ じん か	obstetrics and gynecology
14. 歯科	し か	dentistry
15. 小児科	しょう に か	pediatrics
16. 内用薬	ない よう やく	medicine for internal use
17. 外用薬	がい よう やく	medicine for external use
18. 用法	よう ほう	instructions for use
19. 毎食	まい しょく	every meal
20. 毎回	まい かい	every time
21. 朝食	ちょう しょく	breakfast
22. 夕食	ゆう しょく	supper
23. 3日分	みっ か ぶん	3 days worth
24. ～包	～ ほう	~ pack(s)
25. ～錠	～ じょう	~ tablet(s)

3 NEW CHARACTERS

Seventeen characters are introduced in this lesson. Use the explanations to help you understand and remember the characters. Study the compound words to increase your vocabulary.

病 医 歯 児 産 保 受 付 来 薬 診 察 計 支
払 法 毎

207 病 sickness, illness
ビョウ

一 亠 广 疒 疒 疒 疒 疒 病
病 病

病, which combines 疒 man in bed and 丙 stiff legs, means sickness. 疒 is used as a radical to refer to sickness.

病院	びょういん	hospital
病気	びょうき	sickness, disease
病室	びょうしつ	sickroom
病人	びょうにん	sick person
· · · ◇ · · ·		
急病	きゅうびょう	sudden illness
病名	びょうめい	the name of a disease
大学病院	だいがく びょういん	university hospital
成人病	せいじんびょう	adult disease

208 医 medicine; healing
イ

一 丆 丆 三 呁 医 医

医 combines 匚 box and 矢 arrow (cf. 196 知), referring here to fine needles used in acupuncture. Originally indicating a doctor's box of needles, 医 has come to mean medical science, healing, or medical doctor.

医者	いしゃ	medical doctor
医院	いいん	clinic, doctor's office
医学	いがく	medical science
· · · ◇ · · ·		
外科医	げかい	surgeon
内科医	ないかい	physician, internist
医療費	いりょうひ	medical expenses

209 歯 tooth
は、(ば)、シ

丨 卜 止 止 歨 歨 歨 歯
歨 歨 歯 歯

Formerly written 齒, 歯 combines 止 stop (cf. 150) and a pictograph of the front teeth. Thus 歯 originally suggested stopping food in the mouth by biting it with one's teeth, and now simply means tooth.

歯医者	はいしゃ	dentist
歯科	しか	dental surgery, dentistry
歯科医	しかい	dentist
· · · ◇ · · ·		
虫歯	むしば	decayed tooth
前歯	まえば	front tooth
入(れ)歯	いれば	dentures
義歯	ぎし	artificial tooth, dentures

210 児	infant, child ジ、ニ	丿	刂	旧	旧	旧	児	児	

児 was originally written 兒, which derived from a pictograph of an infant whose head is large and whose skull bones have not yet joined completely.

小児科	しょうにか	pediatrics
小児科医	しょうにかい	pediatrician
	· · · ◇ · · ·	
児童	じどう	child

211 産	give birth; produce う・む、サン	丿	亠	六	六	立	产	产	产
		产	産	産					

産 combines 生 life (cf. 42) and 产 becoming obvious and visible, which comes from a man standing 立 (cf. 167) on a cliff 厂. Thus 産 suggests new life becoming visible, such as giving birth or producing.

産む	うむ	to give birth
産婦人科	さんふじんか	obstetrics and gynecology
	· · · ◇ · · ·	
生産する	せいさんする	to produce
特産品	とくさんひん	special product
土産	*みやげ	souvenir

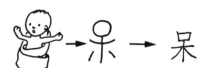

212 保	keep, maintain; protect たも・つ、ホ	丿	亻	亻	亻口	伫	伃	伃	保
		保							

保, which combines 亻 man and 呆 baby wrapped in a shawl, means protect, take care, keep, or maintain.

保証人	ほしょうにん	guarantor
保証書	ほしょうしょ	warranty card
保険	ほけん	insurance
保険証	ほけんしょう	health insurance card
	· · · ◇ · · ·	
保つ	たもつ	to keep, to maintain
保健所	ほけんじょ	public health center
保育園	ほいくえん	nursery school, day-care center
国民 健康保険	こくみん けんこう ほけん	national health insurance

213 受	receive う・ける、ジュ	ノ	イ	彡	爫	爫	严	受	受		

受 combines 彡 hand, 冖 ship, and 又 another hand. Goods carried by ships were received by one person from another, hand to hand, at a port.

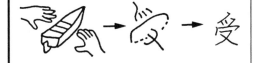

受ける	うける	to receive; to take (a test); to have (an operation)
受(け)取る	うけとる	to receive, to get

· · · ◇ · · ·

受(け)身	うけみ	passive voice
郵便受け	ゆうびん うけ	mail box
受験する	じゅけんする	to take an examination

214 付	attach つ・く、つ・ける、フ	ノ	イ	仁	付	付					

付 represents a hand 寸 attaching a stick 丶 to a man イ.

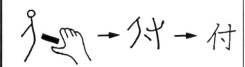

付く	つく	to stick
付ける	つける	to attach, to put, to stick
時間外受付	じかんがい うけつけ	reception before and after office hours

· · · ◇ · · ·

付録	ふろく	supplement, appendix
付属病院	ふぞく びょういん	hospital attached to ~
交付する	こうふする	to deliver / issue (a certificate, etc.)

215 来	come く・る、ライ	一	厂	厄	远	来	来	来			

来 derives from a pictograph of ripe grain ready to be harvested. Since harvest suggests the coming of new crops, 来 means come or coming.

来る	くる	to come
来週	らいしゅう	next week
来月	らいげつ	next month
外来受付	がいらい うけつけ	outpatient reception
外来語	がいらいご	foreign loanword

· · · ◇ · · ·

将来	しょうらい	future
来年	らいねん	next year

216 薬

medicine

くすり、（ぐすり）、ヤク、（ヤッ）

一 十 艹 艹 艹 芍 芍 苩
苩 莦 莃 蒁 菥 薬 薬 薬

薬 combines the radical 艹 plant and 楽, a tree laden with nuts that makes a pleasant sound when shaken. Thus 薬 suggests plants used to make sick people feel better, a form of medicine.

艸 → 屮屮 → 艹
器 → 樂 → 楽

薬	くすり	medicine, drug, pill
内用薬	ないようやく	medicine for internal use
外用薬	がいようやく	medicine for external use
薬局	やっきょく	pharmacy, drugstore
· · · ◇ · · ·		
薬代	くすりだい	medicine expenses
目薬	めぐすり	eye medicine
薬品	やくひん	medicine, chemicals
薬学	やくがく	pharmacology

217 診

diagnose, examine

シン

丶 亠 二 言 言 言 言 訁
訁 訡 診 診

診 combines 言 speak (cf.78 話) and 彡 lots of hair covering 𠆢 a head. Thus 診 suggests a doctor asking a patient lots of questions to cover all his symptoms, in other words, diagnosing him.

休診日	きゅうしんび	vacation day for clinic
· · · ◇ · · ·		
初診	しょしん	the first medical examination
再診	さいしん	medical re-examination
検診	けんしん	medical examination
診療時間	しんりょうじかん	consultation / surgery hours

218 察

investigate; judge; guess

サツ

丶 宀 宀 宀 灾 灾 灾 灾
宨 寂 寥 寥 察 察

察, which combines 宀 house and 祭 festival (cf. 36), suggests purifying a house thoroughly. By extension, 察 now means investigate thoroughly and judge based on investigation. An associated meaning is guess.

診察する	しんさつする	to examine / see a patient
診察室	しんさつしつ	examination / consultation room
診察券	しんさつけん	patient's card
診察日	しんさつび	consultation / surgery day
· · · ◇ · · ·		
警察	けいさつ	police

219 計 measure; total; plan
ケイ

計, which combines 言 speak (cf. 78 話) and 十 add (cf. 184 協), suggests adding up the number of words that a person speaks. From this, 計 has come to mean measure or total.

会計	かいけい	accounts, bill; cashier
時計	とけい	watch, clock
	· · · ◇ · · ·	
計算する	けいさんする	to calculate, to compute
小計	しょうけい	subtotal
合計する	ごうけいする	to total, to add up
計画する	けいかくする	to plan

220 支 branch; support
さ さ・える、シ

支 represents a branch that is held in a hand.

支出	ししゅつ	expenses, expenditure
	· · · ◇ · · ·	
支える	ささえる	to support
支部	しぶ	branch (of a union, association, etc.)
支社	ししゃ	branch office of a company
支持する	しじする	to support

221 払 pay; sweep off
はら・う、（ばら・い）

払 derives from 拂, which combines 扌 hand and 弗 vine being untangled by two sticks (cf. 200 費). Thus 払 suggests sweeping and, by extention, pay (an act of clearing up debts).

払う	はらう	to pay; to sweep off
支払う	しはらう	to pay
支払(い)窓口	しはらい まどぐち	payment window, cashier
	· · · ◇ · · ·	
払(い)込み	はらいこみ	payment
払(い)戻し	はらいもどし	refund, repayment
現金払い	げんきん ばらい	cash payment
分割払い	ぶんかつ ばらい	payment in installments

222 法	law; method ホウ、(ポウ)	丶	⺀	⺘	⺘	⺘	注	法	法

法 combines ⺡ water and 去 pot, indicating a tight-lidded pot that keeps water inside. From this 法 has come to mean law, which limits people's behavior. An associated meaning is method.

方法	ほうほう	method, way
使用法	しようほう	how to use, directions for use
用法	ようほう	usage, instructions for use
文法	ぶんぽう	grammar

· · · ◇ · · ·

法律	ほうりつ	law
法学部	ほうがくぶ	Faculty of Law
調理法	ちょうりほう	how to cook
寸法	すんぽう	size, measurements

223 毎	every, each マイ	ノ	⺊	⻑	勹	毎	毎		

毎 combines ⺊ hair pin and 母, a derivation of 母, which is composed of 女 woman and two dots for breasts and means mother. 毎, which originally also represented mother, has come to mean every, because every mother has a child.

毎日	まいにち	every day
毎回	まいかい	every time
毎食	まいしょく	each/every meal

· · · ◇ · · ·

毎日新聞	まいにち しんぶん	Mainichi Daily News
毎週	まいしゅう	every week
毎月	まいつき	every month
毎年	まいとし／まいねん	every year

4 PRACTICE

I. Write the readings of the following kanji in hiragana.

1. 病院　　2. 病気　　3. 外来受付　4. 会計

5. 支払い　6. 薬局　　7. 診察室　　8. 医者

9. 保険証　10. 外科　11. 内科　　12. 産婦人科

13. 歯科　　14. 小児科　15. 外用薬　16. 内用薬

17. 用法　　18. 毎食　19. 毎回　　20. 医院　21. 医学

22. 歯科医　23. 保証人　24. 外来語　　25. 使用法

26. 歯医者さんに行ったら、きょうは、休診日でした。

27. 受付で、診察券を受け取ってください。

28. 来週、国のともだちが日本へ来ます。

29. この薬を毎日三回のみなさい。

30. さいごに、会計の窓口_{まど}でお金を払います。

Ⅱ. Fill in the blanks with appropriate kanji.

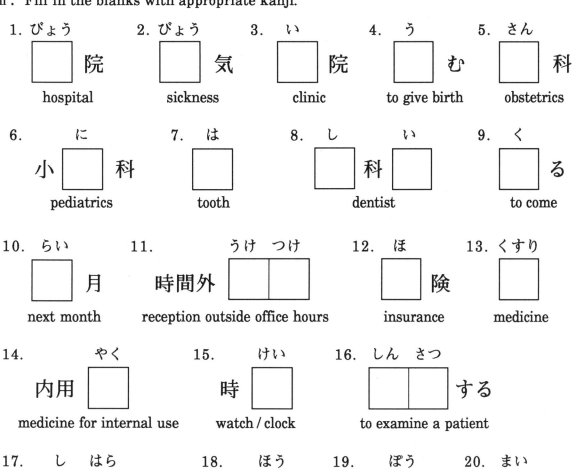

1. びょう ☐院 hospital
2. びょう ☐気 sickness
3. い ☐院 clinic
4. う ☐む to give birth
5. さん ☐科 obstetrics

6. に 小☐科 pediatrics
7. は ☐ tooth
8. し い ☐科☐ dentist
9. く ☐る to come

10. らい ☐月 next month
11. うけ つけ 時間外☐☐ reception outside office hours
12. ほ ☐険 insurance
13. くすり ☐ medicine

14. やく 内用☐ medicine for internal use
15. けい 時☐ watch / clock
16. しん さつ ☐☐する to examine a patient

17. し はら ☐☐い日 the date of payment
18. ほう 方☐ method
19. ぽう 文☐ grammar
20. まい ☐食 every meal

I. The words listed below relate to one of three places: A) the inside of a university building, B) a university campus, or C) a hospital. Group them appropriately and write their letters in the spaces provided.

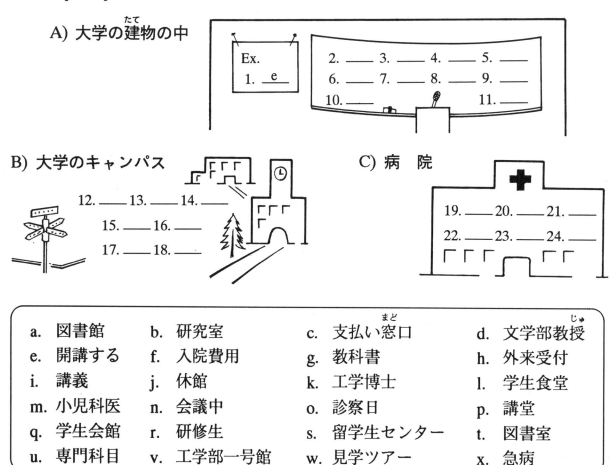

A) 大学の建物の中

Ex.
1. __e__
2. ____ 3. ____ 4. ____ 5. ____
6. ____ 7. ____ 8. ____ 9. ____
10. ____ 11. ____

B) 大学のキャンパス

12. ____ 13. ____ 14. ____
15. ____ 16. ____
17. ____ 18. ____

C) 病 院

19. ____ 20. ____ 21. ____
22. ____ 23. ____ 24. ____

a. 図書館	b. 研究室	c. 支払い窓口	d. 文学部教授
e. 開講する	f. 入院費用	g. 教科書	h. 外来受付
i. 講義	j. 休館	k. 工学博士	l. 学生食堂
m. 小児科医	n. 会議中	o. 診察日	p. 講堂
q. 学生会館	r. 研修生	s. 留学生センター	t. 図書室
u. 専門科目	v. 工学部一号館	w. 見学ツアー	x. 急病

II. Find the missing kanji and write them or their corresponding letters in the spaces below.

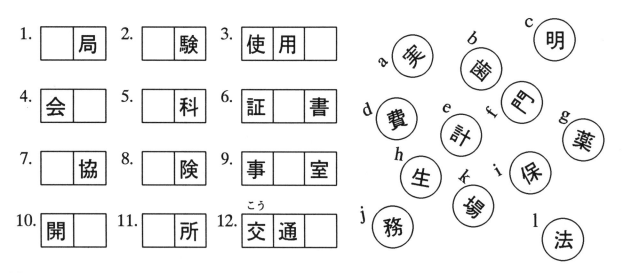

1. ☐ 局   2. ☐ 験   3. 使 用 ☐

4. 会 ☐   5. ☐ 科   6. 証 ☐ 書

7. ☐ 協   8. ☐ 険   9. 事 ☐ 室

10. 開 ☐   11. ☐ 所   12. 交 通 ☐

a. 医   b. 歯   c. 明   d. 費   e. 計   f. 門   g. 薬   h. 生   i. 保   j. 務   k. 教   l. 法

スーパーでセールがあります

DEPARTMENT STORES in Japan carry a wide variety of products, while supermarkets stock mainly food and other daily necessities. For people who prefer smaller, specialized stores, there are butcher shops, fishmarkets, vegetable shops, and so on. Although bargaining is not encouraged, stores do occasionally hold sales. Especially at the end of the seasons, stores carry lots of discount merchandise to attract customers. To save money, look for advertising leaflets in newspapers.

1 INTRODUCTORY QUIZ

Look at the illustrations below and refer to the words in VOCABULARY. Then try the following quiz.

Ⅰ. Read the following advertisement for a supermarket sale, and then choose the correct answers to the questions below.

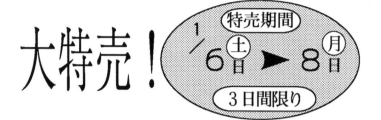

スーパー　大京ストア　＜北山店＞

大特売！

特売期間
1
6日（土）▶ 8日（月）
3日間限り

牛肉、豚肉、鳥肉、ハム・・１割引
魚、さしみ・・・・・・・・３割引
やさい、くだもの・・・・・２割引

このほか食料品は、全品お安くなって
おります。きょうのお買い物は、ぜひ
大京ストア　食料品売り場へ！

営業時間　10:00a.m.～7:00p.m.
定休日　第1、3水曜日

1. この店は、大京ストアの（ a. きたやまみせ　　b. きたやまてん ）です。

2. 6日から8日までは、（ a. 高く　　b. 安く ）売ります。

3. 肉、魚、やさいの中で、一番安くなる物は（ a. 肉　　b. 魚　　c. やさい ）です。

4. さしみは（ a. 肉　　b. 魚 ）売り場で買います。

5. *ハムは（ a. 魚　　b. 肉 ）売り場で買います。　　　　　　　　(*ham)

6. （ a. くつした　　b. コーヒー ）も安くなります。

7. いま、午後5時です。店は（ a. 開いています。　　b. 閉まっています。 ）

8. 毎月、第2、第4水曜日は（ a. 休みです。　　b. 開いています。 ）

Ⅱ. Decide which characters represent the following pictures, and then circle the correct answers.

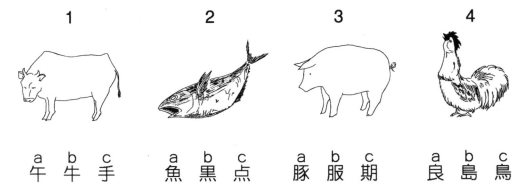

	1			2			3			4	
a	b	c	a	b	c	a	b	c	a	b	c
午	牛	手	魚	黒	点	豚	服	期	良	島	鳥

2 VOCABULARY

Study the readings and meanings of these words to help you understand the INTRODUC-
TORY QUIZ.

1.	スーパー		supermarket
2.	店	みせ	store
3.	北山店	きた やま てん	Kitayama store
4.	大特売	だい とく ばい	super sale
5.	高い	たか い	expensive
6.	安い	やす い	cheap
7.	売る	う る	to sell
8.	肉	にく	meat
9.	牛肉	ぎゅう にく	beef
10.	豚肉	ぶた にく	pork
11.	鳥肉	とり にく	chicken
12.	魚	さかな	fish
13.	1割引	いち わり びき	10% discount
14.	一番	いち ばん	the most
15.	安くなる	やす く なる	to be discounted
16.	物	もの	thing
17.	売り場	う り ば	counter in a shop
18.	買う	か う	to buy
19.	食料品	しょく りょう ひん	groceries, provisions
20.	全品	ぜん ぴん	all items
21.	(お)買い物	（お）か い もの	shopping
22.	営業時間	えい ぎょう じ かん	business hours

23. 開く	あく	to open
24. 閉まる	しまる	to close
25. 第1水曜日	だい いち すい よう び	the 1st Wednesday
26. 定休日	てい きゅう び	Shop Holiday, regular holiday

3 NEW CHARACTERS

Thirteen characters are introduced in this lesson. Use the explanations to help you understand and remember the characters. Study the compound words to increase your vocabulary.

店 売 肉 牛 豚 鳥 魚 割 品 安 買 物 業

---

224 店 shop, store
みせ、テン

店 combines 广 roof or house, ト fortuneteller's stick (cf. 154 外), and 口 space or place. 占 formerly meant selecting and occupying a good place according to the advice of a fortuneteller. 店 thus came to mean a house set up in a place good for business, that is, a shop or store.

店	みせ	shop, store
書店	しょてん	bookstore
開店時間	かいてん じかん	store opening time
閉店時間	へいてん じかん	store closing time
・・・◇・・・		
本店	ほんてん	main store, head office
支店	してん	branch store / office
百貨店	ひゃっかてん	department store
専門店	せんもんてん	specialty store, store specializing in ~

---

225 売 sell
う・る、バイ

売 derives from 賣, which combines 士, a simplified form of 出 take out or show (cf. 108), and 買, which usually means buying (cf. 234), but here means something to do with business. Thus 売 suggests selling. (Imagine a man 士 standing 儿 behind a showcase in a shop 冖.)

売る	うる	to sell
売場	うりば	counter in a shop, vending area
特売	とくばい	special / bargain sale
売店	ばいてん	stand, stall
・・・◇・・・		
大売(り)出し	おおうりだし	big sale
発売日	はつばいび	the day of release for sale
新発売	しんはつばい	newly on sale

226 肉 meat ニク		一	冂	内	内	肉	肉		

肉 derives from a pictograph of meat. When 肉 is used as a part of other kanji, it is written 月.

肉	にく	meat
・・・◇・・・		
×挽(き)肉	ひきにく	minced / ground meat
肉料理	にくりょうり	meat dishes
×焼肉	やきにく	grilled meat

227 牛 cow, bull うし、ギュウ		ノ	′	二	牛				

牛 derives from a pictograph of a cow or bull's head.

牛	うし	cattle, cow, bull
牛肉	ぎゅうにく	beef
・・・◇・・・		
牛×乳	ぎゅうにゅう	cow's milk
牛×丼	ぎゅうどん	a bowl of rice topped with sliced beef
水牛	すいぎゅう	water buffalo

228 豚 pig ぶた、トン		ノ	刀	月	月	月′	月″	肑	肕
		肠	豚	豚					

豕 derives from a pictograph of a pig. 月 meat (cf. 226 肉) was added in order to specify a pig which is eaten, namely, pork.

豚	ぶた	pig
豚肉	ぶたにく	pork
豚カツ	とんカツ	breaded pork cutlet
・・・◇・・・		
×焼豚	やきぶた	roast pork
×酢豚	すぶた	sweet-and-sour pork

| 229 鳥 | bird; chicken
とり、チョウ | ノ | イ | 宀 | 卢 | 皀 | 皀 | 鳥 | 鳥 |
| | | 鳥 | 鳥 | 鳥 | | | | | |

鳥 derives from a pictograph of a bird.

鳥	とり	bird
鳥肉	とりにく	chicken meat
小鳥	ことり	small bird
· · · ◇ · · ·		
焼鳥	やきとり	grilled chicken on a stick
白鳥	はくちょう	swan

| 230 魚 | fish
さかな、（ざかな）、うお、ギョ | ノ | ク | ク | 合 | 角 | 鱼 | 魚 |
| | | 魚 | 魚 | 魚 | | | | |

魚 derives from a pictograph of a fish.

魚	さかな	fish
魚つり	さかなつり	fishing
焼魚	やきざかな	grilled fish
· · · ◇ · · ·		
魚屋	さかなや	fish store
魚市場	うおいちば	fish market
金魚	きんぎょ	goldfish

| 231 割 | divide; proportion
わ・る、カツ | ' | ' | 宀 | 宁 | 中 | 宝 | 宝 |
| | | 害 | 害 | 割 | 割 | | | |

割 combines 刂 sword and 害, a basketlike mask over a mouth, indicating an obstacle. 割 formerly meant cutting an obstacle, and then came to mean divide and proportion. 害 by itself means harm.

割る	わる	to divide, to break, to split
二割	にわり	20%
割(り)引き	わりびき	discount
学割	がくわり	student discount
· · · ◇ · · ·		
割合	わりあい	rate, ratio; comparatively
分割する	ぶんかつする	to divide, to partition

232 品	goods, article; quality しな、ヒン、（ピン）	ノ	口	口	口	口	口	品	品
		品							

品 derives from a pictograph of goods piled up.

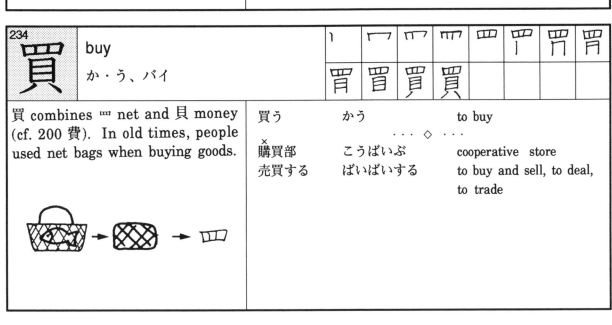

品	しな	goods; quality
品川	しながわ	Shinagawa (place)
食料品	しょくりょうひん	foodstuff, groceries
スポーツ用品	スポーツようひん	sporting goods
全品	ぜんぴん	all items / goods
・・・◇・・・		
品切れ	しなぎれ	out of stock, sold out
食品	しょくひん	food, foodstuff
作品	さくひん	piece of work, product
日用品	にちようひん	daily necessities
電気製品	でんき せいひん	electrical appliance

233 安	peaceful; inexpensive, cheap やす・い、アン	，	ˋ	宀	安	安	安		

安 represents a woman 女 in a house 宀, which suggests a peaceful household. Inexpensive is an associated meaning, perhaps coming from the idea of staying at home and making things oneself.

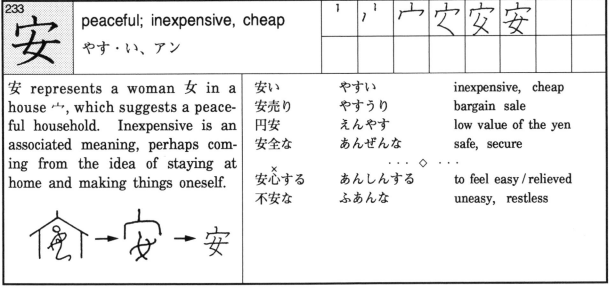

安い	やすい	inexpensive, cheap
安売り	やすうり	bargain sale
円安	えんやす	low value of the yen
安全な	あんぜんな	safe, secure
・・・◇・・・		
安心する	あんしんする	to feel easy / relieved
不安な	ふあんな	uneasy, restless

234 買	buy か・う、バイ	ノ	口	罒	罒	罒	罒	胃
		胃	胃	買	買			

買 combines 罒 net and 貝 money (cf. 200 費). In old times, people used net bags when buying goods.

買う	かう	to buy
・・・◇・・・		
購買部	こうばいぶ	cooperative store
売買する	ばいばいする	to buy and sell, to deal, to trade

235 物	object, thing もの、ブツ、モツ	ノ	㇇	牛	牛	牛	牝	物	物

物 combines 牜 or 牛 cattle (cf. 227) and 勿 elephant's tusks and trunk. The Chinese chose these animals to represent the concept of things.

物	もの	thing
品物	しなもの	goods, article
買(い)物する	かいものする	to shop
見物する	けんぶつする	to sightsee
· · · ◇ · · ·		
忘れ物	わすれもの	things left behind, lost property
動物	どうぶつ	animal
荷物	にもつ	baggage, cargo

236 業	occupation, business ギョウ	'	''	'!'	'''	业	业	业	业
		业	业	業	業	業			

業 represents a musical instrument that is difficult to play, hanging from a rack. From this, 業 has come to mean job or business, which can also be difficult.

工業	こうぎょう	(manufacturing) industry
本日休業	ほんじつ きゅうぎょう	Closed Today
営業中	えいぎょうちゅう	open for business, Open
営業時間	えいぎょう じかん	business hours
· · · ◇ · · ·		
授業料	じゅぎょうりょう	tuition
卒業する	そつぎょうする	to graduate
産業	さんぎょう	industry
職業	しょくぎょう	job, profession

4 PRACTICE

I. Write the readings of the following kanji in hiragana.

1. 北 山 店　　2. 大 特 売　　3. 牛 肉　　　　4. 豚 肉

5. 鳥 肉　　6. 魚　　　　7. 1 割 引 き　　8. 売 場

9. 食 料 品　　10. 全 品　　11. お 買 い 物　　12. 営 業 時 間

13. 定 休 日　　14. 書 店　　15. 特 売　　　　16. 焼 肉

17. 牛　　　　18. 豚 カ ツ　　19. 学 割　　　　20. 品 川

21. 安 全 な　　22. 休 業

23. あの店には、品物がたくさんあります。

24. ケーキをつくりますから、たまごを三つ、割ってください。

25. 安くてよいセーターが買えて、うれしいです。

Ⅱ. Fill in the blanks with appropriate kanji.

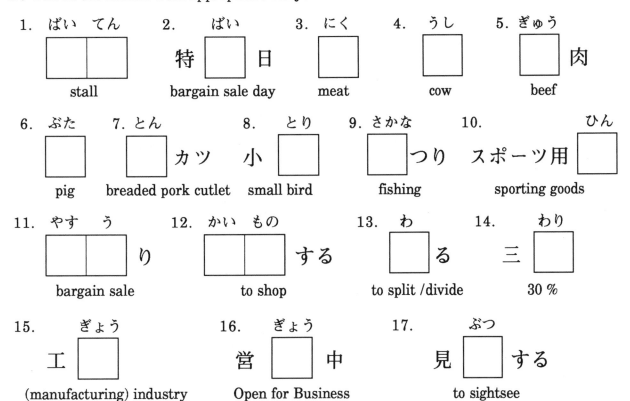

1. ばい　てん
特 □ 日
stall

2. ばい
特 □ 日
bargain sale day

3. にく
□
meat

4. うし
□
cow

5. ぎゅう
□ 肉
beef

6. ぶた
□
pig

7. とん
□ カツ
breaded pork cutlet

8. とり
小 □
small bird

9. さかな
□ つり
fishing

10. ひん
スポーツ用 □
sporting goods

11. やす　う
□ り
bargain sale

12. かい　もの
□ する
to shop

13. わ
□ る
to split /divide

14. わり
三 □
30 %

15. ぎょう
工 □
(manufacturing) industry

16. ぎょう
営 □ 中
Open for Business

17. ぶつ
見 □ する
to sightsee

5 SUPPLEMENT

Sales in a Supermarket

A Sale on a Shopping Street

食堂に入りましょう

AT LUNCH time many restaurants offer low-priced set meals. Japanese noodles or rice dishes served in bowls are an even cheaper and simpler alternative. Japanese tea and water are served free of charge, and in many university and company cafeterias, self-serve machines for cold water, hot water, and tea are available. In this lesson, you will learn how to read words commonly used in cafeterias, restaurants, and menus.

1 INTRODUCTORY QUIZ

Look at the illustrations below and refer to the words in VOCABULARY. Then try the following quiz.

Ⅰ. Restaurants display signs to tell the public if they are open or not. Which of the following signs allows you to enter? Choose the correct answer.

毎度ありがとうございます
準　備　中
a. (　　　)

定　休　日
b. (　　　)

いらっしゃいませ
営　業　中
c. (　　　)

Ⅱ. Read the signs on the tables below, and then choose the correct answers.

1. よやくしてあります。　　　　　(a.　　b.　　c.)
2. たばこをすってもいいです。　(a.　　b.　　c.)
3. たばこをすってはいけません。(a.　　b.　　c.)

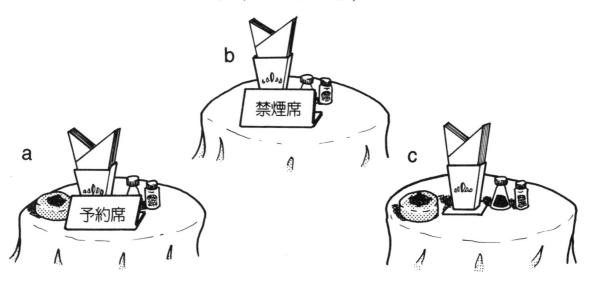

b　禁煙席

a　予約席

c

Ⅲ. Understanding the meaning of kanji in a menu will help you order. While reading the menu on the opposite page, write T if the statement is true and F if the statement is false.

1. (　　) この店の焼肉（やき）は牛肉です。
2. (　　) 牛丼（どん）は定食です。
3. (　　) 豚汁は和食です。
4. (　　) みそ汁は洋食です。
5. (　　) 鳥肉からあげは飲み物です。
6. (　　) こうちゃは飲み物です。
7. (　　) おゆは350円です。
8. (　　) パーテイーをするときは、よやくしたほうがいいです。

MENU

お食事

焼肉定食	（豚焼肉、サラダ、みそ汁、ごはん、つけもの）	1000円
和定食	（焼魚、煮もの、豚汁、ごはん、つけもの）	980円
中華定食	（鳥肉からあげ、マーボどうふ、サラダ、ごはん）	850円
洋食弁当	（エビフライ、コロッケ、サラダ、ライス）	950円
牛丼		450円
天ぷらそば		650円
スパゲッティ		500円

お飲み物

ビール（大）	500円
ビール（小）	300円
紅茶	350円
コーヒー	
ジュース	

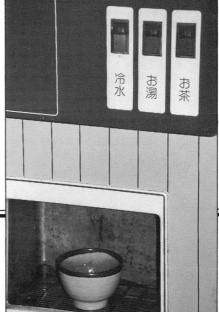

冷水　お湯　お茶

＊パーティのご予約お受けいたします。

In university cafeterias and other less expensive restaurants, you will often find self-service tea, hot water, or ice water free of charge.

Samples from the Menu on the Previous Page

豚汁　　　　　　　　　　に
　　　　　　　　　　　　煮もの

　　　　　　　　　　　　やき
　　　　　　　　　　　　焼魚

和定食　980円

べんとう
洋食弁当　950円

牛　丼

どん
牛丼　450円

サラダ　　つけもの　　みそ汁

ごはん　　　　　　　　　　　やき
　　　　　　　　　　　　　　焼肉

やき
焼肉定食　1,000円

2 VOCABULARY

Study the readings and meanings of these words to help you understand the INTRODUCTORY QUIZ.

1.	食堂	しょく どう	restaurant / cafeteria
2.	準備中	じゅん び ちゅう	Preparing to Open
3.	定休日	てい きゅう び	Shop Holiday, regular holiday
4.	営業中	えい ぎょう ちゅう	Open for Business
5.	予約席	よ やく せき	reserved table
6.	禁煙席	きん えん せき	nonsmoking table
7.	(お)食事	(お) しょく じ	meal
8.	焼肉	やき にく	grilled meat
9.	定食	てい しょく	set meal
10.	みそ汁	みそ しる	*miso* soup
11.	つけもの		pickles
12.	牛丼	ぎゅう どん	a bowl of rice topped with sliced beef
13.	天ぷらそば	てん ぷら そば	*soba* with tempura
14.	鳥肉からあげ	とり にく からあげ	fried chicken
15.	(お)飲み物	(お) の み もの	beverage
16.	中華	ちゅう か	Chinese style
17.	マーボどうふ		*tōfu* with chili pepper
18.	紅茶	こう ちゃ	black tea
19.	(お)湯	(お) ゆ	hot water
20.	(お)茶	(お) ちゃ	Japanese tea
21.	冷水	れい すい	ice water
22.	(ご)予約	(ご) よ やく	reservation
23.	受ける	う ける	to receive
24.	豚汁	ぶた じる／とん じる	*miso* soup with pork and vegetables
25.	和食	わ しょく	Japanese food / meal
26.	和定食	わ てい しょく	Japanese-style set meal
27.	焼魚	やき ざかな	grilled fish
28.	煮もの	に もの	cooked vegetables seasoned with soy sauce
29.	洋食	よう しょく	Western food / meal
30.	弁当	べん とう	meal in a lunch box
31.	エビフライ		fried prawns
32.	コロッケ		croquette

3 NEW CHARACTERS

Ten characters are introduced in this lesson. Use the explanations to help you understand and remember the characters. Study the compound words to increase your vocabulary.

和 洋 汁 飲 茶 湯 予 約 席 備

---

237 和 peace, harmony; Japan
ワ

ノ 二 千 禾 禾 和 和 和

和, which combines 禾 grain (cf. 45 科) and 口 mouth, indicates peace, because eating makes people happy and peaceful. In addition, 和 is often used to mean Japan, because ancient Japan was called 倭, pronounced *wa*.

平和	へいわ	peace
和室	わしつ	Japanese-style room
和食	わしょく	Japanese food / meal
和定食	わていしょく	Japanese-style set meal
	· · · ◇ · · ·	
×和風	わふう	Japanese style
和英辞典	わえい じてん	Japanese-English dictionary
漢和辞典	かんわ じてん	dictionary of kanji in Japanese

---

238 洋 ocean; foreign, Western
ヨウ

丶 丶 氵 氵 氵 汼 洋 洋
洋

洋 combines 氵 water and 羊 sheep's head, meaning beautiful or correct and by extension, splendid and big (cf. 131 着; 188 義). A big, splendid body of water is an ocean. Beyond the ocean, there are foreign lands.

東洋	とうよう	the East, the Orient
西洋	せいよう	the West
洋食	ようしょく	Western food / meal
洋室	ようしつ	Western-style room
	· · · ◇ · · ·	
×太平洋	たいへいよう	the Pacific Ocean
洋書	ようしょ	Western book
洋式	ようしき	Western style
×洋服	ようふく	Western clothes

---

239 汁 soup
しる、（じる）

`	゛	シ	シ	汁			

汁 combines 氵 water and 十 add (cf. 184 協). In order to cook soup, various ingredients are added to water.

みそ汁	みそしる	*miso* soup
豚汁	ぶたじる／とんじる	*miso* soup with pork and vegetables

· · · ◇ · · ·

240 飲 drink
の・む、イン

ノ	ハ	仒	今	今	含	食	食
食	飠ク	飲ケ	飲				

飲 combines 飠 eat or meal (cf. 180 食) and 欠 wide open mouth, and refers to opening one's mouth wide to drink. 欠 by itself means lack or absence.

飲む	のむ	to drink
飲(み)物	のみもの	beverage
飲(み)水	のみみず	drinking water
飲料水	いんりょうすい	drinking water (formal)

· · · ◇ · · ·

飲食店	いんしょくてん	eating house, restaurant

241 茶 tea
チャ、サ

一	十	艹	艹	苂	苂	苂	茶
茶							

茶 derives from 荼. The radical 艹 represents plant, and 余 indicates dividing 八 a piled up 十 mound 亼 to make space, implying extra space, time, etc. 茶 thus means tea (the plant for brewing the drink, or the drink itself), which people enjoy in their spare time.

（お）茶	（お）ちゃ	(Japanese) tea
紅茶	こうちゃ	black tea

· · · ◇ · · ·

茶色	ちゃいろ	brown color
茶道	さどう	art of tea ceremony
喫茶店	きっさてん	tearoom, coffee shop

242 湯 hot water ゆ、トウ	ヽ	ミ	シ	シ	シ口	シ月	シ月	沢
	沢	湯	湯	湯				

湯, which combines 氵 water and 昜 sun rising up high (cf. 197 場), indicates hot water with steam rising up out of it.

（お）湯	（お）ゆ	hot water
・・・◇・・・		
～湯	～ゆ	suffix for bathhouses or hot springs
銭湯	せんとう	public bathhouse
給湯	きゅうとう	hot water supply
熱湯	ねっとう	boiling water

243 予 in advance, beforehand ヨ	フ	マ	豕	予				

予 combines マ crouching man, and 亅 (or 了) which resembles a hanging string tied up with a knot and means complete or finish. From the idea of crouching just before leaping toward a goal, 予 has come to mean in advance.

予定	よてい	schedule, plan
予定表	よていひょう	timetable, written schedule
・・・◇・・・		
予習する	よしゅうする	to prepare one's lessons
天気予報	てんき よほう	weather forecast
予算	よさん	budget, estimate of income and expenses

244 約 appointment, promise; approximately ヤク	く	幺	幺	糸	糸	糸	約
	約						

約 combines 糸 thread and 勹 large spoon. When the ancient Chinese made an appointment, they carved a spoonlike shape into a tree and tied a thread there to mark the place. Thus 約 came to mean appointment.

約～	やく～	about, approximately
予約する	よやくする	to reserve, to book, to subscribe
先約	せんやく	previous appointment
・・・◇・・・		
約束する	やくそくする	to promise, to make an appointment
契約書	けいやくしょ	written contract

245 席 seat, place セキ

一 广 广 广 府 府 府 席
席 席

席 combines 巾 cloth (cf. 147 帳) and 庐, simplified from 庶, which here indicates warm because of 灬 fire (cf. 250 無). Together they suggest a cushion, a place for sitting, or seat.

席	せき	seat
出席する	しゅっせきする	to attend
予約席	よやくせき	reserved seat / table
禁煙席	きんえんせき	nonsmoking seat / table
… ◇ …		
欠席する	けっせきする	to be absent from
優先席	ゆうせんせき	priority seat (for the aged or handicapped, etc.)
自由席	じゆうせき	unreserved seat
指定席	していせき	reserved seat
座席	ざせき	seat

246 備 prepare, furnish ビ

ノ イ イ イ 什 什 伊 伊
俻 俻 俻 備

備 combines 亻 man and 甫, a container in which arrows are placed before being used, and suggests preparing or furnishing something.

準備する	じゅんびする	to prepare
準備中	じゅんびちゅう	in preparation, Preparing to Open
… ◇ …		
設備	せつび	facility, equipment
備考	びこう	remark, note
予備	よび	spare; preparatory, preliminary
予備校	よびこう	cram school

4 PRACTICE

I. Write the readings of the following kanji in hiragana.

1. 準 備 中　　　2. 営 業 中　　　3. 予 約 席　　　4. 禁 煙 席

5. 焼 肉 定 食　6. みそ 汁　　7. 牛 丼　　　8. お 飲 み 物

9. 紅 茶　　　10. お 湯　　　11. 豚 汁　　12. 和 食

13. 焼 魚　　　14. 洋 食　　　15. 平 和　　16. 西 洋

17. 飲 料 水　　18. 予 定　　　19. 先 約

20. 東洋医学は、なかなかよさそうですね。

21. お茶を飲みましょう。

22. パーティーをする時は、予約してください。

23. この席は、あいていますか。

24. 約50名が会議に出席しました。

II．Fill in the blanks with appropriate kanji.

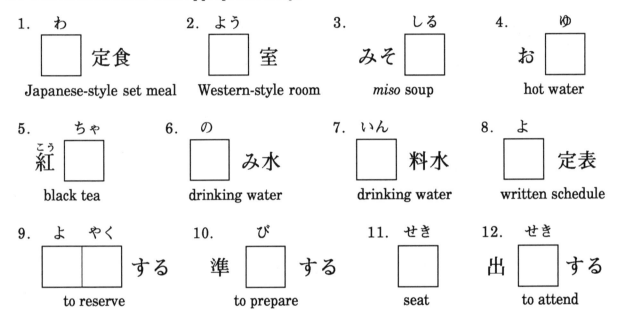

1. わ ☐ 定食
Japanese-style set meal

2. よう ☐ 室
Western-style room

3. みそ ☐ しる
miso soup

4. お ☐ ゆ
hot water

5. 紅 こう ☐ ちゃ
black tea

6. ☐ の み水
drinking water

7. ☐ いん 料水
drinking water

8. ☐ よ 定表
written schedule

9. ☐ よ ☐ やく する
to reserve

10. 準 ☐ び する
to prepare

11. ☐ せき
seat

12. 出 ☐ せき する
to attend

不動産屋で

WHEN LOOKING for a place to live, try visiting a real estate company or looking over a real estate rental magazine. If you have already chosen a location, it will be helpful to visit a local realtor in that district. Realtors typically hang house and apartment listings in the window. Some terms commonly used when searching for housing are technical but important to know. Therefore in this lesson, you will have an opportunity to learn some kanji outside of the 250 basic characters taught in this textbook.

1 INTRODUCTORY QUIZ

Look at the illustrations below and refer to the words in VOCABULARY.

A real estate agent offers information on two apartments, A and B. Compare the two in detail. Which do you prefer?

Apartment A

貸マンション 80,000円

間取り／ワンルーム

所在地／文京区白山3_2

　　　　ハイム白山7F

交通／三田線白山駅歩8分

専有面積／21.5㎡

　　　　（6.5坪）

バルコニー／3.5㎡

構造／鉄筋コンクリート

築年数／14年

特記／エレベーター・冷暖

　　　給湯有り

敷金／160,000円

礼金／160,000円

管理費／3,000円

下駄箱　玄関　MBPS

洗面所

浴室　台所

洋室
（9）

バルコニー

Apartment B

貸アパート
98,000円

間取り／2K
所在地／足立区千住元町
　　　　5ー13
　　　　北都ハウス2F
交通／千代田線・日比谷線
　　　北千住駅バス10分
　　　歩1分
専有面積／25.5㎡
　　　　　(7.7坪)
バルコニー／3.9㎡
構造／木造モルタル
築年数／7年
特記／給湯・シャワー有り

敷金／1ヶ月
礼金／2ヶ月
管理費／無し

下駄箱　玄関　ユニットバス　MU
キッチン
和室4.5畳
押入
和室6畳
押入
バルコニー

After signing a contract, you usually pay your first month's rent, a nominal administrative fee, a security deposit (usually 2-3 months' rent), a gift payment to the landlord (usually 2-3 months' rent), and an agent's fee (usually 1 month's rent). Normal leases are for a period of two years, but it is possible to leave before this time by notifying the landlord and paying a penalty (usually 1 month's rent). Contracts can be renewed after the initial two-year period by making another payment to the landlord (usually 1-2 months' rent).

2 VOCABULARY

Study the readings and meanings of these words to help you understand the INTRODUCTORY QUIZ.

1.	不動産屋	ふ どう さん や	real estate agency, realtor
2.	貸	かし	for rent, for lease
3.	～有り	～ あり	with ～, ～ available
4.	～無し	～ なし	without ～, no ～
5.	間取り	ま どり	arrangement of rooms, floor plan
6.	洋室	よう しつ	Western-style room
7.	和室	わ しつ	Japanese-style room
8.	玄関	げん かん	entry hall
9.	台所	だい どころ	kitchen
10.	浴室	よく しつ	bathroom
11.	洗面所	せん めん じょ	washroom
12.	押入	おし いれ	closet
13.	～畳／帖	～ じょう	counter for tatami mats
14.	交通	こう つう	transportation
15.	歩～分	ほ ～ ふん	～ minutes on foot
16.	専有面積	せん ゆう めん せき	privately owned area
17.	～坪	～ つぼ	counter for 3.3㎡ area
18.	構造	こう ぞう	structure
19.	鉄筋コンクリート	てっ きん コンクリート	reinforced concrete
20.	木造モルタル	もく ぞう モルタル	wood and mortar
21.	築年数	ちく ねん すう	years since constructed
22.	冷暖（房）	れい だん （ぼう）	air-conditioner and heater
23.	給湯	きゅう とう	hot water supply
24.	敷金	しき きん	deposit money
25.	礼金	れい きん	gift money to landlord
26.	管理費	かん り ひ	administrative fee

3 NEW CHARACTERS

Four characters are introduced in this lesson. Use the explanations to help you understand and remember the characters. Study the compound words to increase your vocabulary.

屋 貸 有 無

---

247 屋

roof; house; shop

や、オク

ｺ	ｺ	尸	尸	层	层	层	屋
屋							

屋 combines 尸 cloth covering something and 至 reaching a goal or dead end (cf. 190 室). Thus 屋 suggests a cover for shutting something out, meaning roof or house. An associated meaning is a house of business, namely, a shop.

尸 → 尸

不動産屋	ふどうさんや	real estate agency, realtor
部屋	へや	room
肉屋	にくや	meat shop
屋上	おくじょう	housetop, roof
· · · ◇ · · ·		
八百屋	やおや	vegetable store, greengrocery
屋外	おくがい	outdoor
屋内	おくない	indoor

---

248 貸

lend, rent out

か・す

ノ	イ	仁	代	代	代	代	貸
貸	貸	貸	貸				

貸 combines 代 replace or substitute (cf. 86) and 貝 money (cf. 200 費). When lending or renting something, one receives money in substitution for what is lent.

貸す	かす	to lend, to rent out
貸室	かししつ	room for rent
貸出期間	かしだし きかん	lending period
· · · ◇ · · ·		
貸マンション	かしマンション	apartment for rent
貸切りバス	かしきりバス	chartered bus

---

249 有

exist

あ・る、ユウ

ノ	ナ	才	有	有	有		

有, which combines ナ hand (cf. 89 手) and 月 meat (cf. 226 肉), indicates a hand holding meat to show proof of its existence.

→ → 有

有る	ある	to exist; to have
～有り	～あり	with ~, ~ available
有名な	ゆうめいな	famous, well-known
有料	ゆうりょう	payment required
· · · ◇ · · ·		
有楽町線	ゆうらくちょうせん	Yurakucho Line
有効期間	ゆうこう きかん	the term / period of validity
有効期限	ゆうこう きげん	the deadline for validity

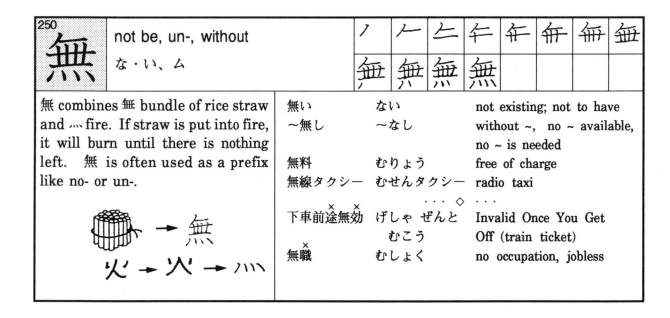

| 250 無 | not be, un-, without | ノ | ┌ | ┌ | 午 | 缶 | 缶 | 無 | 無 |
| | な・い、ム | 無 | 無 | 無 | 無 | | | | |

無 combines 無 bundle of rice straw and 灬 fire. If straw is put into fire, it will burn until there is nothing left. 無 is often used as a prefix like no- or un-.

無い	ない	not existing; not to have
~無し	~なし	without ~, no ~ available, no ~ is needed
無料	むりょう	free of charge
無線タクシー	むせんタクシー	radio taxi
· · · ◇ · · ·		
下車前途無効	げしゃ ぜんと むこう	Invalid Once You Get Off (train ticket)
無職	むしょく	no occupation, jobless

4 PRACTICE

Ⅰ. Write the readings of the following kanji in hiragana.

1. 不 動 産 屋   2. 貸 室   3. ～ 有 り   4. ～ 無 し

5. 台 所   6. 浴 室   7. 押 入   8. 交 通

9. 屋 上   10. 無 料   11. 貸 出 期 間

12. この部屋には、シャワーは有りますが、ふろは無いです。

13. ともだちにお金を貸してあげました。

14. あの方が、有名なブラウン博士です。

Ⅱ. Fill in the blanks with appropriate kanji.

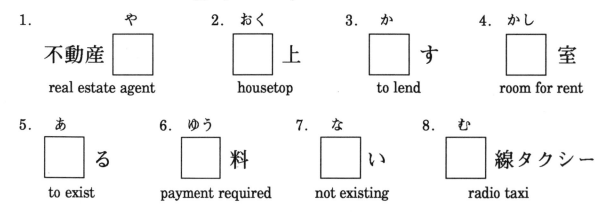

1. や
不動産 [　]
real estate agent

2. おく
[　] 上
housetop

3. か
[　] す
to lend

4. かし
[　] 室
room for rent

5. あ
[　] る
to exist

6. ゆう
[　] 料
payment required

7. な
[　] い
not existing

8. む
[　] 線タクシー
radio taxi

REVIEW EXERCISE Lessons 19–21

I. Find the correct words from the box below and write their corresponding letters in the parentheses.

1. （　）で、いいアパートを見つけました。

2. とんカツは、牛肉ではなく（　）でつくるんです。

3. 日本のお金がよわくなることを（　）といいます。

4. もう（　）なので、買い物をやめなくてはいけません。

5. この道路は（　）ですから、お金を払ってください。

6. デパートに行けば、いろいろな（　）が買えます。

7. （　）にはたいてい、たたみがあります。

8. （　）で定期券を買ったほうが安くなります。

```
a. 物      b. 閉店時間      c. 学割      d. 豚肉

e. 有料     f. 和室      g. 円安     h. 不動産屋
```

II. Many of the 250 kanji you have learned in this textbook have common pronunciations. Shown below are compound words that include examples of this. Write these kanji in the blanks.

1. よう

東 [　] the East

専 [　] for exclusive use

水 [　] Wednesday

2. あん

[　] 内所　information center

[　] 全な　safe

[　] 証番号　secret code number

3. どう

自 [　] automatic

水 [　] tap water

食 [　] dining room

4. かい

[　] 場　meeting place

[　] 速　semi-express train

[　] 始　start

5. こう

[　] 学部　Faculty of Engineering

[　] 空便　airmail

[　] 義室　lecture room

6. けん

危 [　] danger

実 [　] experiment

意 [　] opinion

217

7. じ

□ 故 accident

□ 間 time

□ 分 oneself

8. きゅう

研 □ research

特 □ special express train

連 □ consecutive holidays

9. きょう

□ 都 Kyoto

□ 室 classroom

□ 会 association

10. き

電 □ electricity

日 □ diary

定 □ regular

11. しょう

□ 火器 fire extinguisher

□ 学生 primary school children

□ 月 new year

12. せん

□ 週 last week

□ 門 major field

□ 面所 wash room

13. ふ

□ 通 stoppage of traffic

□ 通 ordinary

14. ぎょう

三 □ 目 the third line

営 □ 中 Open

15. よ

□ 定 schedule

□ 金 money deposited

16. せい

学 □ student

平 □ the Heisei era

17. しん

□ 入生 new student

□ 察券 patient's card

18. ぶん

半 □ half

□ 学 literature

19. し

休 □ pause

都 □ city

20. ぽう

文 □ grammar

一 □ 通行 one way traffic

21. かん

図書 □ library

五日 □ five days

22. やく

予 □ 席 reserved seat

内用 □ internal medicine

23. む

事 □ 所 office

□ 料 free of charge

24. いん

入 □ hospitalization

□ 料水 drinking water

APPENDIX A
Japanese Names
(Some Japanese names using the 250 kanji in this text book)

Family Names

平山	大山	中山	本山	丸山	西山	東山
小山	北山	内山	水田	平田	大田	前田
金田	土田	本田	上田	山田	中田	小田
西田	北田	南田	高田	内田	安田	和田
水口	田口	山口	山本	中本	木下	山下
田中	山中	金子	土屋	大平	本間	田代

ひらやま	おおやま	なかやま	もとやま	まるやま	にしやま	ひがしやま
こやま	きたやま	うちやま	みずた	ひらた	おおた	まえだ
かねだ	つちだ	ほんだ	うえだ	やまだ	なかた/だ	おだ
にしだ	きただ	みなみだ	たかだ	うちだ	やすだ	わだ
みずぐち	たぐち	やまぐち	やまもと	なかもと	きのした	やました
たなか	やまなか	かねこ	つちや	おおひら	ほんま	たしろ

First Names

| (male) | 学 | 正 | 修 | 博 | 洋 | 明 | 正一 |
| | 義一 | 研二 | 洋三 | 文男 | 正男 | 和男 | 安男 |

| まなぶ | ただし | おさむ | ひろし | ひろし | あきら | しょういち |
| よしかず | けんじ | ようぞう | ふみお | まさお | かずお | やすお |

| (female) | 曜子 | 京子 | 文子 | 博子 | 正子 | 道子 |
| | 明子 | 保子 | 洋子 | 和代 | 安代 | |

| ようこ | きょうこ | ふみこ | ひろこ | まさこ | みちこ |
| あきこ | やすこ | ようこ | かずよ | やすよ | |

APPENDIX B
The Main Radicals Presented in This Book and Some Examples

Ⅰ. へん (left part) ▐□

1.	イ	man, people	休、使、住、代、（人）、便、停、他、修、保、付、備
2.	言	word, speak	語、話、証、認、訂、記、講、議、診、計
3.	日	sun	（日）、時、曜、暗、明、（cf. 普、間）
4.	糸	thread	線、絡、終、約
5.	氵	water	（水）、洗、準、注、消、法、洋、汁、湯
6.	金	metal, gold	（金）、鉄、銀
7.	扌	hand	（手）、押、扱、払
8.	阝	wall, hill	際、険、階、院

Ⅱ. つくり (right part) □▐

1.	攵	strike, hit	攻、故、務、教
2.	阝	village	部、都、郵

Ⅲ. かんむり (top part) ▭

1.	艹	plant	薬、茶
2.	宀	roof, house	定、室、実、察、安、（cf. 案、空）

Ⅳ. あし (bottom part) ▭

1.	儿	legs	先、児、（cf. 洗、祝、院、売、見）
2.	心	mind	急、意、（cf. 認、快）

Ⅴ. かまえ (enclosing part) ◱ ▬

1.	門	gate	間、開、門、閉
2.	囗	enclosure	四、団、回、国、図

Ⅵ. にょう (left and bottom part) ◪

1.	辶	proceed	週、込、通、連、速、道

Ⅶ. たれ (top and left part) ◰

1.	尸	corpse	局、届、屋
2.	疒	sickness	病

Ⅷ. その他 (miscellaneous)

1.	木	tree	（木）、本、東、案、業、様、（cf. 休）
2.	土	earth	（土）、地、堂、場、（cf. 煙）
3.	十	add, many	（十）、千、協、博、（cf. 準、計、汁）
4.	口	mouth, box	名、（口）、各、号、右、品、和、（cf. 語、故、知）

APPENDIX C
Kanji Compounds in This Textbook

Ⅰ. Main Types of Compounds and Some Examples

Type 1. Adjective + Noun:
正門、正面、前者、後半、外国、内線、東口、西洋、洋服、和食、全国、全部、各地、各駅、大会、大型、小包、本館、本店、分館、支店、先週、現代、次回、新年、故人、他人、若者、国道、実費、私費、実物、空車、定食、近所、急用、終電、初診、紅茶、冷水、暗室、金魚

Type 2. Verb (Modifier) + Noun:
学者、歩行者、講師、歌手、引力、保証人、証明書、洗濯機、入口、出口、住所、案内所、教室、食堂、会議室、売店、会場、学会、講演会、連絡先、入場券、用法、記事、着物、食品、送料、運賃、来月

Type 3. Adverb + Verb:
外出、外食、予約、予定、予習、予報、中止、中立、代表、実験、実習、実行、厳禁、公認、右折、専用、始発、急行

Type 4. Verb + Noun (Objective):
入国、出国、入学、休講、授業、卒業、入院、退院、開門、開店、閉店、閉館、発音、発車、停車、下車、駐車、見物、買物、読書、禁煙、給湯、消火、預金

Type 5. Pair of Synonyms:
都市、道路、場所、階段、中央、方向、品物、職業、書状、出発、到着、開始、停止、禁止、使用、分割、研究、確認、故障、議論、変更、訂正、正確、平和、平常、危険、部分

Type 6. Pair of Antonyms:
大小、前後、左右、上下、出入、東西、南北、男女、売買、終始、発着、開閉

Ⅱ. Kanji Commonly Used in Compounds and Some Examples

部： 部分、部屋、全部、本部、支部、北部、工学部、文学部
書： 書状、読書、洋書、辞書、教科書、参考書、申込書、証明書、保証書、説明書、案内書、契約書、修了証書
用： 用事、用紙、用法、用意、使用、利用、専用、学生用、外用薬
券： 食券、入場券、乗車券、定期券、回数券、急行券、特急券、指定券、診察券
所： 住所、所在地、現住所、洗面所、案内所、停留所、市役所、区役所、保健所、研究所、事務所、発電所、便所、近所
内： 内科、案内、都内、車内、学内、室内、屋内、年内、家内

線： 営団線、都営線、山手線、新幹線、国内線、国際線、内線、無線
代： 代表、代金、代理人、電気代、薬代、時代、世代、現代
中： 中立、中止、中学、中心、準備中、工事中、会議中、営業中、使用中、一日中
全： 全国、全線、全品、全学、全体、全員、全部、全快
車： 車内、電車、発車、停車、下車、駐車、自動車、自転車、普通車、空車
口： 口座、入口、出口、東口、西口、北口、南口、非常口、連絡口、窓口、人口
出： 出席、出発、出国、出口、出前、提出、輸出
便： 便利、便所、郵便、航空便、船便、宅急便、学内便、定期便、不便
事： 事実、事件、事務、事故、火事、工事、用事、大事、記事、知事
不： 不安、不通、不用、不便、不可、不足、不明、不動産
急： 急行、急用、急病、急停車、準急、特急、救急車
発： 発車、発音、発表、発電所、始発、終発、開発
正： 正式、正門、正義、正常、正確、正解、正月、正面、訂正、修正
記： 記入、記号、記事、記念、記者、日記、暗記、左記
外： 外国、外出、外来、外用薬、外務省、外科、海外、市外、屋外、時間外、意外
常： 通常、平常、正常、日常、非常口
料： 料金、料理、有料、無料、授業料、送料、手数料、資料、調味料
道： 道路、車道、歩道、鉄道、国道、水道、柔道、茶道、片道
者： 学者、医者、記者、歩行者、消費者、経営者、前者、後者
気： 気体、気分、天気、電気、火気、人気、空気
講： 講義、講演、講堂、講師、講座、講習会、開講、休講、受講届
食： 食堂、食事、食券、食前、食後、食間、定食、外食、立食
館： 大使館、本館、分館、別館、学生会館、図書館、一号館、映画館、美術館、博物館、旅館、閉館
会： 会話、会社、会場、会議、会員、会費、会計、会館、社会、大会、学会、国会、講演会、忘年会、研究会、協会、閉会、面会、入会金、記者会見
義： 義理、義務教育、講義、主義、定義、正義、意義
議： 議論、議題、議長、議会、議員、会議、国会議事堂
室： 教室、講義室、五号室、研究室、実験室、図書室、会議室、事務室、診察室、喫煙室、室内、浴室、洋室、地下室、暗室、空室
実： 実物、実用、実習、実行、実験、実際、事実
場： 場内、場合、工場、会場、市場、駐車場、入場券
費： 費用、食費、学費、会費、交通費、医療費、実費、国費、私費
法： 法律、法人、法学部、文法、用法、使用法、調理法、寸法
店： 書店、開店、閉店、本店、支店、売店、百貨店、専門店、飲食店、喫茶店
品： 品物、全品、食品、食料品、用品、作品、日用品、電気製品、非売品、特産品、薬品
洋： 洋食、洋室、洋書、洋式、洋服、東洋、西洋
予： 予約、予定、予備、予習、予報、予算
席： 出席、欠席、座席、空席、予約席、自由席、指定席、優先席、禁煙席、喫煙席
屋： 屋上、屋外、屋内、部屋、肉屋、八百屋、魚屋、不動産屋

APPENDIX D
Answers to the Quizzes

第一課 ： 1 - 470　　2 - 930　　3 - 500　　4 - (3902) 5791
　　　　　　5 - 省略 (Omitted)　　6 - 省略 (Omitted)

第二課 ： Ⅰ. 1 - c　　2 - b　　3 - b　　4 - b　　5 - b　　6 - b　　7 - c
　　　　　　Ⅱ. 1 - 12がつ 25にち　　　2 - 1がつ なのか　　　3 - 2しゅうかん
　　　　　　4 - 12がつ 15にち、4がつ ついたち

第三課 ： 1 - へいせい　　2 - よっか、いつか　　3 - げつ、か、すい　　4 - 4　　5 - 5
　　　　　　6 - きん　　　7 - ど　　　　　　8 - 8 or 13　　　　　9 - げつ、きん

第四課 ： 1 - a　　2 - a, b　　3 - b　　4 - b　　5 - a　　6 - b, a

第五課 ： Ⅰ. 1 - 六本木、東京　　2 - 9, 5, 12, 4　　3 - 8900　　4 - スミス　　5 - a

第六課 ： Ⅰ. 1 - f　　2 - c　　3 - d　　4 - a　　5 - b　　6 - e
　　　　　　Ⅱ. 1 - c, d, e, f　　2 - a　　3 - b, e　4 - e
　　　　　　Ⅲ. 1 - a　　2 - b　　3 - b

第七課 ： Ⅰ. 1. a - 190　　b - 120　　c - 160　　d - 150
　　　　　　　　2. a, d
　　　　　　Ⅱ. 1 - d, b　2 - e　　3 - c

第八課 ： Ⅰ. 1 - a　　2 - a　　3 - b　　4 - a

第九課 ： Ⅰ. 1 - c　　2 - f　　3 - e　　4 - a
　　　　　　Ⅱ. 1 - b　　2 - a　　3 - b　　4 - b　　5 - a

第十課 ： Ⅰ. 1 - a, e, g　　2 - b　　3 - f　　4 - d　　5 - c
　　　　　　Ⅱ. 1 - 5:00　2 - 0:03
　　　　　　Ⅲ. 1 - a　　2 - b　　3 - b　　4 - a

第十一課 ： Ⅰ. b, a
　　　　　　Ⅱ. 1 - D　　2 - A, C　3 - F　　4 - E　　5 - B

第十二課 ： Ⅰ. a - 130　b - 70　　c - 110　d - 50　　e - 270
　　　　　　Ⅱ. 1 - a, b, c, e　　　　2 - d

第十三課 ： Ⅰ. 1 - a　　2 - b　　3 - b　　4 - c　　5 - b　　6 - c　　7 - b

第十四課 ： 1 - a　　2 - b　　3 - b　　4 - b　　5 - c

第十五課 ： 1 - a, a, b　　　　2 - a, b　3 - b　　4 - b　　5 - a　　6 - a, a　7 - b

第十六課 ： Ⅰ. 1 - a　　2 - b　　3 - b　　4 - b　　5 - a　　6 - b
　　　　　　Ⅱ. 1 - a　　2 - a　　3 - b
　　　　　　Ⅲ. A. 講義室、　事務室、　会館、　休講
　　　　　　　　B. 研究室、　実験室、　番号、　一番、　一階、　一号室

第十七課 ： Ⅰ. 1 - 新しい都市　2 - 11号館　　　3 - 二番教室　　4 - 2月24日

Ⅱ. 1 - 3月7日　　　2 - 3,000円　　　3 - 申込書、山本研究室
　　4 - 3月1日　　　5 - はい、行けます。

第十八課　：　Ⅰ. 1. 1) - d　　2) - c　　3) - b　　4) - a
　　　　　　　　 2. 1) - b　　2) - c　　3) - d　　4) - a
　　　　　　Ⅱ. 1 - b　　2 - b　　3 - b　　4 - b　　5 - a, b

第十九課　：　Ⅰ. 1 - b　　2 - b　　3 - b　　4 - b　　5 - b　　6 - b　　7 - a　　8 - b

　　　　　　Ⅱ. 1 - b　　2 - a　　3 - a　　4 - c

第二十課　：　Ⅰ. c
　　　　　　Ⅱ. 1 - a　　2 - a, c　3 - b
　　　　　　Ⅲ. 1 - F　　2 - F　　3 - T　　4 - F　　5 - F　　6 - T　　7 - F　　8 - T

第二十一課：　省略 (Omitted)

Answers to the Review Exercises

Lessons 1 - 5 ：　Ⅰ. 1 - d　　2 - e　　3 - b　　4 - k　　5 - i　　6 - g
　　　　　　　　　　 7 - o　　8 - l　　9 - c　　10 - f　　11 - a　　12 - h
　　　　　　　　　　 13 - p　　14 - n　　15 - j　　16 - m
　　　　　　　　Ⅱ. 1 - b　　2 - a　　3 - b　　4 - a　　5 - a　　6 - b
　　　　　　　　　　 7 - b　　8 - b　　9 - a

Lessons 6 - 10 ：　Ⅰ. 1 - a　　2 - h　　3 - j　　4 - e　　5 - b　　6 - c
　　　　　　　　　　 7 - i, n　8 - f, k　9 - d, g, l, m　　10 - s　　11 - r
　　　　　　　　　　 12 - t　　13 - q　　14 - o
　　　　　　　　Ⅱ. 1 - e　　2 - c　　3 - i　　4 - b　　5 - j　　6 - g　　　7 - a

Lessons 11 - 14：　Ⅰ. ① - c　　② - k　　③ - a　　④ - g　　⑤ - e　　⑥ - d
　　　　　　　　　　 ⑦ - h　　⑧ - j　　⑨ - f　　⑩ - i　　⑪ - b
　　　　　　　　Ⅱ. 1 - a　　2 - a　　3 - b　　4 - a　　5 - b　　6 - a

Lessons 15 - 18：　Ⅰ. 1 - e　　　　A) 2 - 11,　b, d, g, i, k, n, r, t, u, w
　　　　　　　　　　　　　　　　　B) 12 - 18,　a, j, l, p, q, s, v
　　　　　　　　　　　　　　　　　C) 19 - 24,　c, f, h, m, o, x
　　　　　　　　Ⅱ. 1 - g　　2 - a　　3 - l　　4 - e　　5 - b　　6 - c
　　　　　　　　　　 7 - h　　8 - i　　9 - j　　10 - f　　11 - k　　12 - d

Lessons 19 - 21：　Ⅰ. 1 - h　　2 - d　　3 - g　　4 - b　　5 - e　　6 - a
　　　　　　　　　　 7 - f　　8 - c
　　　　　　　　Ⅱ. 1 - 洋、用、曜　　2 - 案、安、暗　　3 - 動、道、堂　　4 - 会、快、開
　　　　　　　　　　 5 - 工、航、講　　6 - 険、験、見　　7 - 事、時、自　　8 - 究、急、休
　　　　　　　　　　 9 - 京、教、協　　10 - 気、記、期　　11 - 消、小、正　　12 - 先、専、洗
　　　　　　　　　　 13 - 不、普　　14 - 行、業　　15 - 予、預　　16 - 生、成　　17 - 新、診
　　　　　　　　　　 18 - 分、文　　19 - 止、市　　20 - 法、方　　21 - 館、間　　22 - 約、薬
　　　　　　　　　　 23 - 務、無　　24 - 院、飲

On-Kun Index

The words in this index are taken from the kanji charts. *On-yomi* in katakana and *kun-yomi* in hiragana are followed by the kanji, their lesson numbers, and serial numbers. Hiragana after (·) indicates *okurigana*. Modified readings in ( ) follow after original readings.

【あ　ア】

あいだ	間	2 -	17
あ・う	会	15 -	183
あか・るい	明	17 -	205
あ・く	開	5 -	73
	空	12 -	158
あ・ける	開	5 -	73
あず・かる	預	11 -	135
あず・ける	預	11 -	135
あたら・しい	新	6 -	92
あつか・う	扱	11 -	149
あと	後	2 -	22
あぶ・ない	危	14 -	171
あら・う	洗	9 -	116
あ・る	有	21 -	249
ある・く	歩	13 -	164
アン	案	9 -	114
	暗	11 -	138
	安	19 -	233

【い　イ】

イ	意	13 -	169
	医	18 -	208
い・きる	生	4 -	42
い・く	行	7 -	104
いそ・ぐ	急	10 -	125
いち	市	4 -	52
イチ	一	1 -	1
（イッ）	一	1 -	1
いつ・つ	五	1 -	5
い・れる	入	4 -	53
いわ・う	祝	3 -	35
イン	引	11 -	134
	院	17 -	201
	飲	20 -	240

【う　ウ】

ウ	右	14 -	177
うえ	上	6 -	93
うお	魚	19 -	230
う・ける	受	18 -	213
うご・く	動	7 -	100
うし	牛	19 -	227
うし・ろ	後	2 -	22
うち	内	6 -	84
う・まれる	生	4 -	42
う・む	産	18 -	211
う・る	売	19 -	225

【え　エ】

エイ	営	6 -	90
エキ	駅	5 -	70
エン	円	1 -	12
	煙	14 -	175

【お　オ】

オウ	央	7 -	96
おお・きい	大	4 -	37
オク	屋	21 -	247
おし・える	教	17 -	198
お・す	押	11 -	136
おとこ	男	5 -	67
おもて	表	10 -	129
お・わる	終	10 -	130
おんな	女	5 -	68

【か　カ】

か	日	2 -	15
カ	火	3 -	27
	科	4 -	45
	下	6 -	81
カイ	開	5 -	73
	回	7 -	105
	快	10 -	127
	会	15 -	183
	階	16 -	187
（ガイ）	階	16 -	187
ガイ	外	12 -	154
か・う	買	19 -	234
か・く	書	5 -	64
カク	各	10 -	121
（カッ）	各	10 -	121
カク	確	11 -	140
ガク	学	4 -	38
（ガッ）	学	4 -	38
か・す	貸	21 -	248
かた	方	8 -	109
（がた）	方	8 -	109

【か　カ（続）】

カツ	割	19 -	231
ガツ	月	2 -	14
（ガッ）	月	2 -	14
かね	金	3 -	30
から	空	12 -	158
から・む	絡	7 -	98
か・わる	代	6 -	86
カン	間	2 -	17
	館	15 -	182

【き　キ】

き	木	3 -	29
（ぎ）	木	3 -	29
キ	期	5 -	60
	記	11 -	146
	気	14 -	170
	危	14 -	171
ギ	義	16 -	188
	議	16 -	189
きた	北	9 -	112
キュウ	九	1 -	9
	休	2 -	13
	急	10 -	125
	究	16 -	192
ギュウ	牛	19 -	227
ギョ	魚	19 -	230
キョウ	京	4 -	40
	協	15 -	184
	教	17 -	198
ギョウ	行	7 -	104
	業	19 -	236
キョク	局	12 -	152
き・る	着	10 -	131
（ぎ）	着	10 -	131
き・る	切	12 -	153
（きっ）	切	12 -	153
（ぎっ）	切	12 -	153
キン	金	3 -	30
	禁	13 -	166
ギン	銀	11 -	133

【く　ク】

ク	九	1 -	9
	区	4 -	56

Vocabulary Index

The words in this index are taken from the vocabulary lists and kanji charts in chapters 1-21.